D1375241

About the author

Maggie Peters is a Transpersonal Psychology psychotherapist, accredited with the United Kingdom Council of Psychotherapists. Central to her transpersonal approach is the belief that within every human being there is a source of wisdom that can be tapped by exploring dreams.

Maggie has been working with her own dreams for the last 20 years and as a dreamwork therapist for 15 years. She is in private practice in Stroud and Bristol, England, and is the originator of Transformative Dreamwork, which provides workshops, seminars and programmes in personal development, as well as professional training for therapists.

Transformative Dreamwork draws upon many sources of inspiration, including the work of C. G. Jung and many 'Jungians', such as Dr Marie-Louise von Franz and Barbara Hannah, along with the ancient dreamwork traditions and rituals of tribal peoples of many cultures. The stories and courage of the many people who have used this approach to transform their lives give continuing, daily inspiration and affirmation as her work develops.

drear

d r e a m w o r k

using your dreams

as the way to self-discovery

and personal development

Maggie Peters

Gaia Books

a gaia original

Books from Gaia celebrate the vision of Gaia, the self-sustaining living Earth, and seek to help its readers live in greater personal and planetary harmony.

 ®

This is a Registered Trade Mark of Gaia Books
an imprint of Octopus Publishing Group
2–4 Heron Quays, London E14 4JP
Copyright © 2005 Gaia Books
Text copyright © 2005 Maggie Peters

The right of Maggie Peters to be identified as the author of this work has been asserted in accordance with Sections 77 and 78 of the Copyright, Designs and Patents Act 1988, United Kingdom.

All rights reserved including the right of reproduction in whole or in part in any form.

First published in the United Kingdom in 2001 by Gaia Books Ltd

ISBN 1-85675-257-7
EAN 9 781856 752572

A catalogue record of this book is available from the British Library.

Printed and bound in China

10 9 8 7 6 5 4 3 2 1

I'd like to dedicate this book to two wise women, Joan Swallow, guide, mentor and friend, who was present when I first set foot on this path and has inspired and unfailingly supported my inner journey from its first faltering steps; and Johanna Timson, the sister I never had, whose gifts of compassion and gentleness and skills in working with the inner child have so enriched my life and work. I am deeply, eternally grateful to both, and offer them my heartfelt thanks and love.

Maggie Peters

contents

part I *Waking up to your dreams*

part I *Introduction*

We are so much more than we know. Our dreams come to remind us of this night after night, each one a message inspired by an indwelling source of bright intelligence that retains an awareness of all that we are and may become. This benign force, which many have called the Dream Maker, takes everyday experiences, weaves them through with unrealized subliminal meaning, imbues the whole with our hidden feelings, and fashions it into the stuff of dreams. Transcending the limitations of the logical, sequential mind, the Dream Maker speaks to us in the language of imagery, symbol, and metaphor, expressed and at times lived by the body, mind, emotions, instinct, and intuition. It wants to hear our soul sing.

Since time began, people have searched for meaning in all of life. This restless searching spans both personal and collective concerns, as we try to understand our own lives and find our place in the world. We have a wealth of ancient tradition within our culture that could support us in this search, but it is lost to many of us. We have been seduced away from it by the desire for instant gratification, the lure of the soundbite in place of reflective consideration, the demands of the material world, and the huge advances in scientific and technological development. Yet the Dream Maker remembers, and can gain access to everything we need to restore us to a sense of our true selves. When we are willing to respect our dreams, to learn the language and put our new knowledge to use in our daily lives, then we strike our individual note, create an authentic way of being, and begin to sing our unique song.

This awakening to ourselves through the dream is for many a kind of homecoming, a remembering of something long forgotten, that brings a great sense of expansion to our lives. Within the realm of the dream, as in the best fairy tales, too, transformation comes and the 'magic' restores to us our birthright.

I came untutored to dreamwork 20 years ago, at a time of personal crisis. Living in rural England, reeling from the sudden loss of my partner, home, and job, I felt completely unsupported. My only sense of identity seemed to be that of a penniless single parent, the last thing I'd ever wanted or anticipated. I had no money for counselling or workshops, which could perhaps have helped, but a defining moment came one day as I was browsing in a bookshop.

I was alone in the philosophy and psychology section, when a book literally shot off a shelf and landed at my feet! Synchronicity, the art of meaningful coincidence, was a fairly new concept to me, but, my curiosity aroused, I picked up the book. It was called *The Dream Makers*, written by Californian psychologists Dr Richard Corriere and Dr Joseph Hart, now long since out of print. It was a book not unlike this one, containing several dreamwork exercises that the reader could use alone.

With all the upheaval in my life, my dreams had become disturbed, full of painful images of abandonment, failure, and isolation. I saw the possibilities, bought the book, and remain deeply grateful to its authors to this day.

For the first few years, I used my dreams to help understand my own inner processes, seeking ways to rebuild my life, with no thought of communicating any of my insights to others. I like to think that it may be because friends and acquaintances witnessed changes in me that they began to share their dreams and invite me to lead them in dreamgroups and workshops.

Seeking to deepen my knowledge of the psychology behind the dream, I took a thorough training course in transpersonal psychology, and became a psychotherapist while gradually evolving my own Transformative Dreamwork approach. My work expanded to include residential workshops and part-time courses of between one and three years' duration for those who wish to walk the way of dreams, either for themselves or in a professional capacity.

My primary influences, along with the transpersonal psychology approach, have been Carl Jung, founder of analytical psychology, and dream pioneer Roberto Assagioli, who created psychosynthesis (a transpersonal branch of psychoanalysis). The great contemporary transpersonal thinker, psychologist, author, and dreamer James Hillman has also been highly influential.

I value equally the mythologies of the great cultures of the world and the ancient dreamwork traditions and rituals of many tribal peoples. Indeed, my own early work was inspired by what I read in *The Dream Makers* about the Senoi people of Malaysia, a tribe of indigenous Indians who live in the jungles of that area. Though surrounded by warring tribes, they are seldom attacked and are reported to be a remarkably peaceful, cooperative people.

The British anthropologist Herbert Noone, documenting his studies of the Senoi in 1939, recorded that other tribes were afraid to attack them, fearing their powerful 'magic', the essence of which is a deep devotion to the study of dreams. They begin their day by sharing their dreams, including those of the children. They then take time to discuss the messages of the dreams in relation to daily life. Finally, they decide what actions to take as a result. The Senoi dreamworkers are described as being very advanced in psychological maturity, in a way unequalled by many other peoples.

Herbert Noone's findings were brought into question by some of his contemporaries who suggested that he had invented the Senoi myth to publicize his own research. This was never proved, but I am glad I did not hear those voices of dissent until after I had begun to trust in dreamwork. Wherever it comes from, even if it was invented, the so-called Senoi way of working with the dream is highly effective.

The Transformative Dreamwork method of blending primitive, classical, and twentieth-century dream traditions yields many rewards, experienced in many areas of life. Improving your relationship with yourself spills over into your relationships with others. The effects of dreamwork may be felt within the family, your place of work, in deepening friendships, sexual relationships, your own creativity, and your existing capabilities.

About this book

This book follows the same experiential approach as my training courses. It does not analyse unduly, nor interpret, but invites the dreamer to engage fully with events, characters, symbols, or anything present in the dream. You will find within these pages not just a collection of techniques, but a multi-faceted approach that is structured yet extremely subtle, sensitive yet highly effective, building a strong connection with your innate creativity and wisdom. Exercises are offered to help you build up skills in working with the dream, and at the same time you will develop a greater awareness of your own attitudes, habitual behaviour patterns, unresolved feelings, and unrecognized potential.

I will introduce many techniques which will teach you a complete approach to the dream. For instance:

• You will learn how to go into a dream while remaining open and allowing, developing an ability to accept what you find without judgement or censorship.

• You will work at establishing boundaries in setting a time limit to your work or protecting yourself when you feel threatened.

• You will discover how to create a sacred space for your dreamwork and to respect the wisdom of the dream. To hold a focus, refusing to be distracted and led away from the point of each exercise.

• You will realize there is a time to speak and a time to stay silent – a time to act and a time to wait.

• You will come more into your own authority, pleasing other people less often, and becoming more integrated or whole.

As you do all of these things, you will learn something of the psychology behind the dream. This understanding gives you the confidence and the will to find more of yourself, developing inner relationships with various aspects of your personality and starting to take that ability into all of your waking relationships. You will begin to make changes, mostly changes of attitude, and develop more compassion for yourself and others. You will begin to heal some old wounds; to learn to accept yourself, knowing that you are fine just the way you are. We all have a shadow side, and we need to find the balance between denial and acting out our darker impulses. No one is perfect and it's okay just to be human. You will learn that vulnerability is a great strength. This knowledge in itself can be deeply empowering.

The dream journey

Beginning with the dream content and the responses evoked, then moving wherever the dream leads, you will learn to make connections between present and past, dream and waking experience. In this way, you can seek out ways of bringing your new knowledge into everyday life. In time, you will be able to translate gained insight into action, and find more effective, appropriate ways of responding to challenging situations.

This is a highly interactive handbook, mirroring your own interaction with your unique dreams. If you merely read it, skimming over the exercises, you will miss out on a great deal. It is your own dreaming and subsequent work that will give you a living experience of dreamwork. The depth of your discoveries, even in the early chapters, may surprise you.

In choosing to read this book, you are saying 'yes' to making a great journey. Following your dreams is a quest for inner wisdom, and every step may take you down an unknown road, into previously uncharted territory. Take it seriously, for it may have a profound effect upon your life. The purpose of this book is to act as a travelling companion, providing a map and a guide; one that knows the territory and has also travelled the terrain.

Some thoughts before you begin

You may like to pause for a moment now, visualizing yourself standing at a threshold in your life. Start by looking behind you at the imaginary landscape through which you have recently travelled. How does it seem to you now? Has this been a difficult journey for you? Were there parts that you particularly enjoyed? How much of it have you travelled alone?

Now take stock of where you are at present, at this place of symbolic threshold. What sort of place is this? What feelings does it evoke for you? You may feel the need to rest here for a while.

When you feel ready, take a look at the journey that lies before you. Is this a different landscape, or more of the same? How far ahead can you see? Are there any obstacles in your way? What would you need to begin such a journey?

Imagine now that you can have everything you need to equip you on the first few steps of your personal journey. How does it feel to be ready to travel: exciting; nerve-racking; joyful; or perhaps 'nothing special'?

The dream journey will, I hope, lead you back to yourself and into a recovery of the true Self. Of course this takes time and persistence. Don't give up and don't give in to despair, impatience, or cynicism. Stay with it; this work truly is worthwhile. A student of mine once said, 'There is good in this work and we can take the good…and use it in our lives'.

When you are ready, turn the page, and you will be on your way!

one 1 | *Starting out*

Almost everyone has a memorable dream that intrigues them. It may be a recent dream, but just as often it is one that occurred long ago, perhaps as far back as early childhood. When I meet people socially for the first time and they learn of my work, it is this dream that they want to share spontaneously. As they do so, something remarkable happens. Instantly, the vibrant energy of the dream manifests itself in the telling, having lost none of its potency over the years. The sharer becomes animated by the quality of this energy, polite conversational gambits are abandoned, and we are drawn into a much more meaningful connection in the imaginal world of the dream. Depending upon the nature of the dream, it will be told with a sense of awe, fearful unease, wonder, or a kind of excitable curiosity as the dreamer once again begins to experience something of the original emotional response. As the dream ends, I am asked the inevitable, 'Now tell me, what on earth does that mean?'.

There's usually some surprise when I reply that I really don't know! People who come across dreamwork casually may expect to be told what their dreams mean. They are fascinated when I suggest that they themselves might try engaging with the dream. I am not in the business of interpreting dreams, but may well comment on the strong effect of the dream, which indicates that it still has significance for the dreamer. We might, if appropriate, consider what questions this person may ask of the dream later on when they are alone, to enable them to elicit the true meaning for themselves. By working with our own dreams, we are able to have unique insights, gaining confidence in developing new skills and perceptions, rather than allowing ourselves to depend on the interpretations of others, however well meaning they may be.

Types of dreams

What is it about some dreams that causes them to lodge so firmly in our memory and to continue to baffle us, often for years to come? Hardly anyone ever quotes a dream that simply re-enacts everyday occurrences, yet if we choose to work with such material, we quickly recognize that every single dream carries a relevant message, and each one is just as important as the more impressive images we all love to share.

The people who choose to come into dreamwork very quickly come to recognize this. Some come out of curiosity, a kind of, 'I did yoga last term, don't know anything about dreamwork, I'll try that' impulse. Others are aware that there are aspects of their life that make them feel uneasy, though they may not be clear exactly why. Some have a particular difficulty they want to work through and feel their dreams are already connecting with this. Whatever brings people in, sooner or later their dreams will take them into their woundedness.

We all carry a wound, a legacy of the human condition. What we fail to realize is just how this old hurt can condition our present life, affecting our choices and unnecessarily limiting our experiences. Because of this, we pay great attention to feelings and emotions in this approach. Once people realize that their most shameful feelings can be valued and well received, there is less need for habitual denial and pretence. This apparent vulnerability can then begin to be recognized as a great strength. It takes courage to reveal our wound in this way, even to ourselves, but it is a first step in the empowerment that the work brings. Often it leads to feelings of relief and release, a sense of inner spaciousness and unaccustomed ease.

Following the dream, helping people to help themselves and find ways of healing their wounds, watching them grow in self-assurance and grace is one of the most satisfying things in my life. Even those who are initially the most fearful and reluctant find their perseverance hugely rewarding.

Let's look now at some of the types of dreams these people have explored as they trod the dreamwork path.

Archetypal dreams

These encompass many 'big dreams'. This term was coined by the eminent psychologist Carl Jung, who recognized during the course of his work that not all dreams are purely personal. Some seem to come from beyond the self. These dreams carry a powerful emotional charge and at times draw upon a kind of knowing which goes beyond our personal or family experience and history. They are drawn from the collective unconscious, which Jung described as '…an immense reservoir of historical memories, a collective memory wherein is preserved, in essence, the history of all humanity' (from *CG Jung Speaking*). This is the home of the archetypes, each one an image for a great force of energy concerned with a type of human behaviour. Archetypes intensify the colours of our lives, bringing long-forgotten layers of meaning to enrich our current experience.

The archetypal Feminine, for instance, may be represented in her universal aspect as Virgin, Mother, or Crone, each one a face of the Triple Headed Goddess, one of the earliest trinities found in almost all cultures. Personalized, she may show her face in dreams as an Innocent Child, the idealized Good Mother, or a Wise Woman. But she has many more than three faces, and each also has a negative, more frightening aspect.

A type of masculine energy may take the form of the Green Man, associated with the great pagan god Pan. He comes to remind today's 'civilized' men of the Wild Man within, who can lead them away from rational, conscious thinking patterns, back into their bodies and their strong connections with the earth. The Green Man may stride into a dream as a being who cannot tolerate confinement. He will rattle the bars of the cage of convention, disrupting routine and structure. Perhaps he will come disguised as the Old Man of the Woods, who can teach men the old ways, luring them away from the computer, out into nature, and deeper into nurturing themselves.

These energies can feel larger than life, as in the nightmare, for instance, which we will now look at, along with some of the common types of 'big' dreams that arouse our curiosity even as they unsettle us (we will return to archetypes in chapter six).

Nightmares

Familiar to all of us, these are strong or shocking dreams that usually come when something has gone amiss in our lives. Just as they can literally shock us awake, so they come to 'wake us up' to what is going awry. There may have been many more subtle signs previously, in waking events or in other dreams, which we have failed to recognize, or chosen to ignore. Then the Dream Maker sends us something that cannot fail to get our attention! However frightening it seems, each nightmare is a gift. It is a symbolic message and needs to be understood and taken seriously. Such dreams seem to be showing us our worst fears, and can leave us with a sense of dread. In fact, mostly the nightmare symbolically depicts something that has already happened!

A sad but wise dream was related to me by Emma, an attractive and fastidious young woman, who had to have a colostomy operation. While she was in recovery, she had the most terrible nightmare. In this, her little dog, which she loved dearly, was run over in the street outside the house and left mutilated in the gutter, where her owner found her. Emma wept bitterly as she related this dream, saying repeatedly:

'How could anyone do that to such a lovely little creature? I'm afraid to let her out of the house, in case the dream is a warning!'

When I asked about the dog's injuries, it transpired that they were to the abdomen. 'Her guts were just spilling out,' Emma explained.

We considered this, along with the dog being found in the gutter, and the strength of her emotional response. Clearly the pet dog represented Emma in the dream, its body suffering a similar trauma to the one she had undergone as a result of her operation. By facing up to this in the dream she was able to begin to accept her illness, and to feel and express its devastating effect. Through her compassion for her dog, Emma found compassion for her own suffering. Having placed the nightmare in this context, she could also let go of her fear for her dog.

We are skilled at cutting ourselves off from painful feelings when difficult events take place, and nightmares may simply be trying to establish a healthy reconnection with appropriate feelings, however disturbing they may be. Working with nightmares can also help us to find new ways of behaving in frightening situations. Many of these terrifying dreams first take place in early childhood, when we first realize our total dependence on our parents, or those who look after us. These adult carers may feel relatively powerless and defenceless themselves, in the face of a specific threat. Sometimes, it is an abusive parent or carer who threatens the child. A small child needs a safe and secure environment at the stage of ego development when it starts to recognize itself as separate from the parents. Many fears can come in at this time, leading to the repeated nightmares, which are the three-year-old's 'night terrors'. Our childhood nightmares may be re-experienced when we find ourselves in situations that bring similar feelings to us as adults.

In *The Dream Makers*, Corriere and Hart tell us how it is when a Senoi child wakes from a nightmare. Instead of dismissing it as 'just a dream' the parent will take it seriously and, while comforting the little one, will ask:

'What has frightened you, my child?'

The child may reply, 'I was walking through the jungle and I heard a noise behind me and a tiger was chasing me!'

The father might well ask, 'What did you do, son?'

'I screamed and ran away as fast as I could!' the child may answer in reply.

'That was a good thing to do, my son. But remember this is your dream and you do not have to be afraid. If it should happen again, just turn around and face that tiger, knowing you can have anything – and anyone – you choose with you as a helper, and you can say to that tiger, "Stop! What are you doing in my dream? Do you know that you are frightening me? What is it that you want from me?"'

Imagine how this technique would empower a frightened child, giving them a sense of their place in the world and encouraging self-respect and confidence. Just knowing that we can have dream helpers to assist us can inspire us to call them up spontaneously when we are in need of support during our nightmares. I have seen it happen many times, even with people who didn't believe in the concept at first.

Let us look at an example: supposing, within a dream, you find yourself wandering, lost and alone in a strange and hostile land. Do you know that you can invite a native of that country, someone who has the skills and knowledge to survive there, to come in as your dream helper? This doesn't mean that you have to visualize how this person might look and behave. Simply put out the call, and appropriate help will come.

Just knowing that this is a possibility can help. For instance, a woman new to dreamwork was able to stop herself at the beginning of a frightening sequence in a recurring dream. She found herself thinking, 'Maggie says I don't have to do this!'. Immediately, a tall confident man appeared at her side and led her through the difficult situation. When she felt afraid, she buried her head in his shoulder and, for the first time, she got through the dream without fear. Later, she told me that she had never had the dream again.

Such work is the continuation of an ancient tradition. In Greek mythology, there are many examples of the hero, about to make his journey, finding the all-important helpers he needs. When Theseus was about to go into the labyrinth to fight the Minotaur, Ariadne gave him a ball of thread so that he might find his way out again. Perseus had his shield to reflect the image of Medusa, so that he could slay her without the risk of meeting her gaze and being turned to stone. But you don't have to be a hero – victims have their helpers too. When Andromeda was chained to the rock, as a sacrifice to the sea monster, waiting to be devoured, it was Perseus that freed her. Many myths offer creative examples of ways of dealing with 'nightmare situations'. Just reading mythology opens the door to our own inner creative imagination, which works for us, asleep or awake.

Recurring dreams

These have much in common with nightmares, in that they are an attempt to fix our attention on some aspect of our lives that does not support our growth. They are usually less shocking, but puzzling in their familiarity, and can be quite distressing as we find ourselves repeating the same actions in a similar setting, time and time again.

These dreams come to show us our hidden anxieties and fears. They demonstrate how we repeat ourselves, often behaving out of habit, unaware of how we get into certain situations, of their affect, and seemingly incapable of changing anything for the better. Such a dream will often occur a night or two after we have unconsciously allowed ourselves to get caught yet again in a relationship or situation that causes us to 'lose ourself' in some way, or to behave 'out of character'.

If you experience dreams like these, look back carefully over what has been going on in your waking life in the few days before the dream. Try to find similar events, feelings, relationships, or conversations. The recurring dream is nudging you to become aware of your habitual behavioural patterns, and to find other more effective and appropriate ways of being.

Pre-cognitive dreams

Such dreams may, at one level, leave us with a perplexed feeling of déjà vu, particularly when quite trivial waking events mirror what has taken place earlier in one of our dreams. Sometimes they present a disturbing and challenging situation, when for instance someone dreams of a terrible plane crash just prior to such a tragedy taking place somewhere. At such times the dreamer is often left with feelings of guilt: 'I should have been able to do something to prevent it!'

Usually there is nothing that could have been done, as the image might apply to any flight, any airline, at any time, anywhere in the world. It can be unnerving to realize that you have psychically 'tuned in' to an actual event prior to its happening. It may help you to think of your psychic abilities as being somewhat randomized, rather like a radio that occasionally picks up another station when you are trying to locate your usual frequency. It may be that some of us have exceptionally well developed intuition, or 'sixth sense', enabling us to perceive images of events outside of our normal time and space continuum. There are no rational explanations for such things. Perhaps this sensitive state is more prevalent when we 'get out of our own head', when our conscious mind is not in control. This can happen when we are asleep and dreaming, or at moments of reverie, for these flashes of premonition can occur out of the blue in waking too. I feel that long ago, when we were in the early stages of evolving, we all had the capacity to presage events, and that we need not be alarmed if occasionally we recapture some of that ability.

Symbolic dreams

The subject of endless fascination, these are a richly creative expression, a way of valuing something that is perhaps overlooked or taken for granted. A symbol always represents much more than is at first apparent, and speaks to us at an instinctual level. For instance, a scythe will carry universal symbolic meaning through association with the ancient Greek god, Cronos, also known as Old Father Time, or the Grim Reaper. For past generations of farmers, it would probably also represent hard work and traditional methods, while for a modern farmer, it may signify a backward step. Almost anything can become a symbol in our dreams, from a pebble to a star, but whatever the generally understood meaning, it will be overlaid with connections from our personal experience.

These dreams can be beautiful or terrible, but they stay with us, exerting a fascination. We may not understand them, but we sense their worth. We need to learn to savour the symbol, and to find its place within our waking lives. Chapter five gives some guidance on working with symbols in dreams.

Wondrous dreams

These are inspirational and can fill us with awe and humility, reminding us of our true place within the universe. They may offer breathtaking spiritual imagery and healing messages, create an overwhelming experience of the beauty of nature, or show us the earth from a perspective only gained from outer space. In these dreams we can fly like a bird, swim like a fish, travel through rocks, or commune with dolphins, unicorns, and dragons. They can also release great creativity when we try to describe them, or bring a deep inner peace as we meditate upon the images.

Valuing your dreams

The archetypal 'big dreams' described are interspersed with more mundane ones that we find less easy to value and remember. But even the shortest or apparently most boring dream carries a message. We don't have to wait for a Steven Spielberg-type dream to carry out dreamwork! However, we do have to discipline ourselves to receive every dream as if it has something significant to say.

Dreams don't come to tell us what we already know, but to show us something deeper. Our tendency to cling to the first perception as if it were the only one may cause us to overlook worthwhile insights. We need to cultivate an attitude of 'this, and this, and this,' rather than 'either this or that'. It is just as important to record the shorter dreams, small snippets or fragments, or even single images, in full, and to work with them as well as with the longer ones that capture our attention so dramatically.

As we return to our dreams to work with them, we must remind ourselves that in dreamwork nothing is fixed and certain, everything changes, and things are not always what they seem. The nightmare can become a great gift, as can the recurring dream that reminds us of our anxieties and may also help us to find ways to deal with them. A dream symbol can inspire an appreciation of some of the extraordinary aspects of our lives. In dreamwork, there is no right or wrong, just different ways of being and of doing things. There are no absolutes, but many creative possibilities. We have to learn how to become open to our true self, and to accept whatever we find in the dream. Following the way of the dream may take us along familiar routes, but enable us to see things in a different light. Alternatively, we may find ourselves exploring an entirely new landscape!

Preparing to work with dreams

Having read this far, it is now time to begin meeting your dreams and recording them. You should do the exercises that follow in sequential order, chapter by chapter, so that your conscious mind can make steady progress through the intrigues and complexities of dreamwork. Keep slow, and safe, and strong.

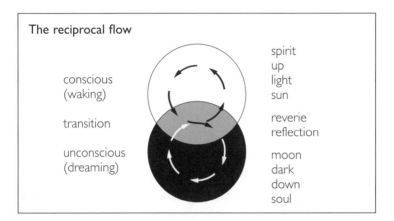

The reciprocal flow

conscious
(waking)

transition

unconscious
(dreaming)

spirit
up
light
sun

reverie
reflection

moon
dark
down
soul

It may help you to imagine the unconscious as a vast realm of which little is known. This realm has its own laws that we must respect if we venture there. It is often symbolically represented as a dark place, located somewhere below us, making a descent necessary if we are to enter. This can unnerve us, as we sense instinctively the power and the dangers inherent in such a place. We are right to be cautious, but if we tread carefully, we need not be afraid. After all, every night as we go to sleep, we relinquish consciousness, yielding through weariness to the unconscious. As we sleep we journey through this realm, creating the images, sensations, symbols, situations, and characters that we remember as we wake. We move effortlessly through this natural cycle of waking, sleeping, dreaming, and waking again, this time bearing something from the unconscious as we return. Isn't this wonderful? We are all experienced in this art, but we don't travel knowingly, we just do it! An integral part of the Transformative Dreamwork approach involves developing the ability to choose consciously to enter different levels of consciousness, so that we may amplify and develop our understanding of the gifts of the dream.

Since our culture no longer values the dream, we have forgotten our dreamwork traditions and lost the finely honed skills that once enabled us to remember and respond to our dreams, according them a place of honour and respect in the world. We have to recreate these skills now, drawing upon old ways of working with dreams, but rendering them appropriate to the twenty-first century.

First of all, we need to provide for ourselves a place of transition between the conscious and the unconscious, sleeping and waking. The diagram on the previous page shows the reciprocal flow as we descend through sleep each night, gathering dream material that we then bring back and acknowledge with our conscious mind. Giving this attention to the dream stirs something within the unconscious to respond to when we next sleep, giving us a subsequent, related dream.

The shaded area represents the transition point, the place where we pause to meet the dream, keeping enough conscious awareness to anchor us, so that we don't drift and lose ourselves in the dark. This place might be seen as being lit by the gentle, diffuse light of the moon, which, though beautiful, makes things less clear and more difficult to define. Familiar things look different by moonlight, changing our perceptions. In this reflected light, the dream holds a mirror for us, affording a glimpse of some aspect of ourselves. Then we can carry with ease what we learn from the dream upwards into the light of the sun, into waking consciousness. There we can recognize where to place our new knowledge, and choose how we may use it. Keeping a dream journal will also help you bring your dreams into waking consciousness.

Creating your dream journal

A dream journal is a notebook or scrapbook of sorts that will soon become very precious to you. It holds your dreams, the thoughts and feelings you have about them, any associations that may arise, work done using the exercises in this book, pictures, symbols, and poems perhaps. A dream journal naturally develops into an intimate autobiographical record that is intensely personal. You may not want anyone else to see it, partly because it will be too revealing and partly because you will be trying out new forms of expression which could leave you feeling vulnerable if held up to scrutiny by others. Try to find a safe place to keep it.

Experiment with personalizing your journal by decorating the cover in some way, with a dream symbol or something else that carries meaning for you. Even just covering it in attractive wrapping paper makes a difference. If you like drawing, there are books with alternate ruled and plain pages that may suit you. Or you may prefer a large ring binder file and notepad instead, so that drawings, articles, and other memorabilia can be included easily. Let your journal be as lively as your dreams! If your current mood is more sombre, with the colours muted and low-key, allow your journal to reflect that. Just find whatever feels right for you.

To help you to record your dreams, you will need to keep your journal and a pen within easy reach of your bed at night. Then you won't have to get out of bed to find them, which can lead to losing the dream. It may be wise to make a change of morning routine, too. Diverting your attention into yoga, meditation, making tea, or having a bath before you write out your dream may mean forgetting part of the dream details.

If your dreams wake you in the night, you have a choice of whether to wake properly to write out the whole dream, or to just make key word notes, hoping to be able to flesh out the dream in the morning. Sometimes this approach works, and at other times it doesn't. By trial and error, see what works best for you, and suits your lifestyle. Sleeping alone presents no problems in this respect, but sitting up in bed with the light on recording your dreams at 3a.m. may call for some negotiation with your partner! Using a torch or flashlight may be more considerate, and less disturbing, or if available, a small battery-powered light that clips onto your journal. Some people prefer speaking into a hand-held tape recorder, then writing out their dreams later. Take a little time to find a way of working that suits you.

As far as possible, try to write in the present tense. Using the past tense distances you from the dream even as you try to recapture it. Writing 'I am' is much more immediate and dynamic than the reminiscent 'I was'. Allow yourself to write fully and smoothly. It is astonishing sometimes to realize, with hindsight, how little of the dream experience you have actually recorded!

Giving each dream a title can be a real time saver later on, when you are moving backwards and forwards, identifying dream themes, symbols, and characters. Glancing at a title means you don't have to read every dream in full. A title crystallizes what is happening in the dream, and what feels significant for you. It is important to date each dream entry, too. The dream is so numinous and elusive that an essential task in these early stages is building a good, appropriate container to help hold the energy of the dream. In many ways this is symbolic, but keeping a dream journal is a practical example of using a little structure and order to shape the container.

Exercise one: waking orientation

• Take your pen, and your dream journal, and begin by asking yourself the following questions. Write down the answers as your first journal entry. Spend no more than twenty minutes on writing.

• What do you hope to gain from dreamwork? What brings you to dreamwork at this time in your life? Are you looking to understand or resolve specific areas, such as: relationships; finding a sense of purpose and direction; coming to terms with a loss of some kind; getting your life back on track after an illness; or perhaps releasing your creativity?

• Does a feeling of more general dissatisfaction or being stuck prompt you to want to work with dreams? Are you feeling beaten down, finding that old ways of being no longer support you? Are you just plain curious? Have you already done some dreamwork, and are you ready for an approach that will give more depth?

Remembering dreams

We have a better chance of remembering our dreams if we can wake up naturally. A strident alarm clock or loud radio alarm can jolt us too suddenly into wakefulness, allowing us no transition time in which to connect tentatively with the experience of the night. Needless to say, a two-year-old child bouncing energetically on your bed will have the same effect! It is not always easy to achieve fifteen or twenty minutes of uninterrupted time to recall and write out your dreams. You may need to just snatch a moment or two to jot down key words or phrases to help hold the dream until you can come back to it later to write it up in more detail. Try telling yourself each night that you are going to wake up fifteen minutes before the alarm goes off, so that you have time for your dreams. You can do it if you really want to, and waking a little earlier is not a lot to give to such a potentially rewarding new interest. Try this next exercise tomorrow morning, upon waking. You will need your journal and a pen.

Exercise two: receiving the dream

• As you wake, just lie quietly for a moment or two, inviting your dreams in. At times the dreams are strongly, immediately present as we wake up. But often we feel we've forgotten them. When this happens, spend a while just connecting with your body.

• How does it seem: relaxed or tense; rested or weary? Are there any particular areas of discomfort or unease?

• Next, tune in to your feelings. How is your mood? Maybe you feel an inexplicable sense of anxiety or dread, or perhaps of lightheartedness or wellbeing? These feelings may well come to rest in the body, seeking expression there. Can you feel 'butterflies in your stomach' or tightness in your chest or throat? In general, how is your body this morning?

• Now move on to your thoughts. What is filling your mind right now? Do you drift slowly into thinking about your day? Are you instantly fully awake? Is your mind already racing ahead, planning your day? If you are already fully alert, try asking your mind to just step aside for a little while, as you reconnect with your dreams.

• By the time you have checked these things out you may have remembered a dream. If not, write in your journal of your experience of the night. How well or badly did you sleep? What (if anything) disturbed you? Record how your body, feelings, and mind responded to this unaccustomed morning consultation.

Be patient! After all, your dreams have been there for you, night after night, since childhood, and you may well have paid them little or no attention. It is hardly surprising if your psyche takes a little time to register this new surge of interest! If you are having difficulty remembering your dreams you might like to try some of the suggestions in the following exercise:

Exercise three: remembering

• Before you go to sleep, spend a little time reviewing your day. What happened to you today? What memorable moments are you left with? Who did you meet? How did you get on with them? Were there challenges, criticism, successes, or praise? How did it affect you, practically and emotionally? How did you respond: reasonably or irrationally, with understanding or in confusion? How does all that leave you feeling now, looking back? With hindsight, might you have acted or reacted rather differently? What good things can you take from the day? Focus on these things as you settle down to sleep.

• Begin to think about the last dream you recalled. Though you may not understand it yet, you can be sure it contains a wealth of information about some aspect of your life. Thank it for being there for you, and invite in the next dream.

• Ask for a dream as you settle down to sleep. Simply send out the thought, or emphasize it by writing a note and putting it under your pillow. Asking three times determines your intent to work with your dreams, and three is traditionally regarded as a magic number (fairies grant three wishes!).

• Find yourself a talisman: a small, natural object that can be particular to dreamwork. Choose something simple and beautiful which feels good to you. Holding it in your hands, affirm your intent to remember your dreams and ask the talisman if it will help you to do this. Keep it by your bed and hold it for a little while when you are ready to go to sleep. Reach out to hold it again as you wake up and let it bring your dream to you.

• Devise a simple dream-recall ritual of your own to carry out each night just before going to sleep, or every morning as you wake.

• If all of this does not produce the desired effect, you should begin to consider what is blocking you: who, or what energy, is within you that does not want you to remember your dreams, even though you have made a start, and feel willing to make the journey?

The dialogue with the Self

As we approach the end of this first chapter, it may be clear that working with our dreams is leading us into a dialogue with the whole Self. Explained simply, our ego holds the energy of the little self, connected with the persona, the way we present ourselves to those we meet, and indeed the person we think ourselves to be. Yet our dreams speak to us of who we truly are. One way they do this is to help us to see how we behave in relationship with others. The characters in our dreams may well be people we know, or know of in waking and in part the dream may be telling us something about that person. But it may equally be using that individual to show us something of an unrealized inner aspect of ourselves.

So the men in a woman's dreams, and in her waking life, may be demonstrating the attitudes and behaviour of her animus, a Jungian term for the inner man who carries the masculine energy in every woman. Similarly, when men dream of women they may be unknowingly getting acquainted with their anima, or inner woman. Authority figures may carry some of the attributes of our inner parents. The children of our dreams can lead us to connect with our inner child. This child may be joyous, playful, abandoned, wounded, whatever. We all carry many symbolic 'children' within, cameos of ourselves at different ages, each holding its own particular energy and way of being.

Some of these symbolic personalities appearing in our dreams will have the capacity to be negative and destructive, while some will be positive and supportive. Most of us have an inner judge, critic, censor, or saboteur, who is always ready to undermine our confidence and thwart our attempts to achieve our goals. As you progress through dreamwork you will begin to recognize people in your dreams who behave in this way. Strangely, our inner defender can have this effect too, seeing potential threats and danger where none exists.

Each of us also has a wise man or woman within; a good mother or father who can offer encouragement and love. These personalities may come into our dreams as our real, outer parents, as older people we respect for their positive qualities, or as completely unknown dream figures.

We need to get to know all of these dream characters who can lead us into greater self-awareness, but we must also learn to become aware of how we respond to them, as this can be equally revealing! As we do this, we begin to develop our inner observer, who can help us to find balance and harmony in dream and waking relationships.

Do you begin to see how our dreams show us that we are much more than we know? It is this expanded sense of being which leads us into the Self. We begin to stretch our boundaries a little, freeing ourselves from habitual ego-based attitudes and allowing another part of us to have a voice.

We need to be gentle with ourselves at such times of change. There may be much ego resistance, but there's no point in giving yourself a hard time. It helps if we can learn to step aside from any negative, critical, or despairing responses that take us away from dreamwork and self-growth. With practice we learn to develop a detached but caring and compassionate inner observer, one who can put things into perspective, becoming a mediator of this process.

Other ideas for self-support

Try to allow a place for any unaccustomed emotions that may move through you as you recognize the messages your dreams bring. This doesn't mean taking out your anger on those around you, or looking for someone else to comfort you if you're feeling sad. You can be alone to thump a cushion or have a good cry. Then take some time to reflect upon what has upset you. Has this sort of thing happened to you before? Did you have the same response? Might the reaction be stronger than the incident actually warrants, suggesting that an old wound is still in need of healing? Accept the experience, and write it all in your journal, which can become your confidant and friend.

Light a candle when you sit to do your dreamwork. This association with light invites in spirit, creating a sense of a sacred space that helps you to hold the focus of the Self. Invite a friend to do dreamwork with you. Then, as your mutual understanding grows, you will each have someone to share with, and can support each other. Remember to accord your friend the same compassion and sensitivity that you have for yourself. All of this contributes to the building of a symbolic container for your inner process, and I promise you it gets easier with practice!

Give yourself a little treat from time to time – you deserve it. It takes courage and persistence to get to know yourself, and begin to live more fully. Acknowledge your courage and persistence and reward yourself. (Some of us need reminding, or to be given permission to indulge ourselves a little.) Give yourself time! Set aside an hour a day for dreamwork, and make it a priority.

Working to gain self-awareness can be exhausting! When you feel you've done enough, put on some soothing music and take a long, warm, aromatic bath, or go for a quiet walk. This will not only relax you, but will also give an opportunity to digest what you've learned, an essential aspect of dreamwork.

Remember this work moves between body, feelings, mind, and spirit. In Western societies we rely heavily on the mind, to the point where it can become quite despotic! There may be times when you want to set your mind aside, creating a space for the emotions, instinct, and spirit. Allow space and time for your spirit to come in. Spend a little quiet time in some favourite tranquil spot, take a walk in the countryside, look at a tree, meditate, or do some yoga.

Reflections on chapter one

Now that you have reached this stage, pause to reflect on the work you have done so far. What emotions, anxieties, fears, or happinesses has this work evoked? Remember that feelings have a place in our lives, and that they will pass. Don't worry if there are things you don't understand – you are only just beginning. It is enough for now to value your dream life and allow it to surprise you at times.

two The dream landscape

When we are new to dreamwork we somehow expect to grasp the meaning of a dream instantly by looking at the wide picture of the whole dream. Our interest may go to a particular part of the dream but, by looking at it on its own, we lose the value of the overall context. Part of that context is the dream setting, or environment.

Our inner Dream Maker is very subtle. Each dream comes as a complete package and everything is significant. Nothing is there by chance. Through this book, I hope to teach you to recognize the significance of your dream material. When you realize that the true and full meaning of a dream lies in the detail, it becomes easier to focus your attention. Take it on trust for the moment, until your own experience gives you the confirmation you need.

The dream setting is so often taken for granted or overlooked in favour of more dramatic events, yet, far from being irrelevant, it has a great deal to tell us. When we go to the theatre the sets are designed to provide an appropriate environment for each scene. As the curtain rises, a mood is created by what we see. So it is with each dream. For instance, the following dream setting is highly evocative: *'I am in a beech wood, just before sunset. The huge orange ball of the sun still casts some warm light through the trees. The air is sweet with the musky scent of the undergrowth and full of birdsong. Though the thick carpet of beech mast muffles the sound of my footsteps, I don't really want to move around and disturb the cathedral-like atmosphere of the wood.'*

The next has a totally different, neutral mood: *'The whole dream is just one scene that takes place in a building society or bank. I am there with my husband but we're sitting on opposite sides of a table or counter. Everything is very cool and formal, mostly grey — the walls, carpet, his suit. Nothing much seems to be happening.'*

Try something for yourself now. Remembering your most recent dream, just for a moment or two imagine it as a movie or play with yourself as a member of the audience. From this place you have disengaged a little from the dream and can begin to observe it. Try to focus on the setting, nothing else. What do you see? Even before any action, what type of setting has been created?

Don't let yourself be distracted by the other people and events in the dream, or by any impatient or dismissive thoughts you may have. This may be your inner censor or critic at work (see chapter three to find out more about the censor). Just see what you can learn from the setting alone. It can be difficult to hold the focus at first, but this will become easier with practice.

You will probably find that thinking about a particular part of your dream generates all sorts of connections, associations, and feelings. Spending some time working with these can give you an insight into at least part of the dream message. We will follow this pattern of observing and noting our responses as we work with each exercise.

The dream environment can give a sense of place, which may or may not be familiar to you. It also gives a sense of time, for instance the period of the 'movie' or 'play' setting may well take you back to a particular time in the past. This often leads to a strong emotional connection, showing how you felt about what was happening to you in that place at that time. One example of such a dream was recounted by Ian, a man in his fifties, who attended one of my dreamwork courses.

'I'm walking up a hill in the rain. I'm in a street of old terraced houses, their front doors opening onto the pavement. It's dark, winter, early evening. A boy about four or five years old is standing on the step at the front door of one house, waiting to be let in. I walk past thinking he must be cold and wet through. He's only wearing short trousers and a short-sleeved shirt.'

Pausing to look at this dream setting, Ian recognized the street as being remarkably like the one where his grandmother lived when he was a small boy. He found the image atmospheric, and described his dream environment further:

'The street was cobbled, lamplight glinting on the wet stones and puddles. It was a steep hill, hard for a young child to climb. The street was empty except for the little boy and me.'

At this point in his dreamwork process, Ian began to feel concern for the child in his dream. *'The people in the house don't seem to know he's there. It's as if they've forgotten about him! What's a child his age doing out at night on his own, anyway?'*

Then Ian paused as he realized… *'That boy could be me! That's how I used to feel when I was left at my gran's. Left out. Always on the outside, not knowing how to fit in!'*

We can see how returning to the dream environment reminded Ian of the mood of his grandmother's place. This in turn led him to remember how he'd felt when his mother left him there for long periods. His well-meaning grandmother used to send him out to play with the other children in the neighbourhood. He felt banned from the house, and yet as an only child he didn't mix easily. He missed his mother and didn't have the social skills to ease his way into new friendships.

At the time of this dream Ian had just started a new job, and had found himself in the position of being the only newcomer in a well-established group. This was an uncomfortable situation for him. The dream gave him the chance to realize how the insecure child within him was once again being activated emotionally because of these familiar, though long-forgotten, feelings.

In further dreamwork he went on to befriend the child, realizing he was too small to reach the doorknocker. Here Ian's inner parent figure (we all have one!) stepped in quite naturally, evoked by the boy's plight. Going back into the dream in his imagination, Ian knocked at the door for him, ushered him into the house, and explained to the grandmother how the boy was feeling.

Ian later said he felt this piece of dreamwork had helped enormously with his difficulties at work. He had been in danger of behaving childishly, feeling the others were unfriendly and deliberately shutting him out. How does this process work? We'll take a closer look over the next few pages.

The dreamwork process

Beginning by observing the setting, we can see how Ian's associations led him into childhood memories and feelings. This, in turn, evoked sympathy and concern for the young boy. By now Ian had a secure emotional connection with the dream. Following through from this, he chose to go back into the dream using a technique called 'active imagination' to help the child.

This technique enables us to go back into the dream, keeping an edge of waking consciousness, to 'dream the dream on' in a beneficial way. By using this approach, Ian began to build a relationship with his inner child, offering help where previously there had been none. Even one small action like this can have a healing effect on the wounded child we all carry within.

We will be looking at this way of working in chapters three and four, and you'll begin to use active imagination in part three of the exercise later on in this chapter. For now, it is enough for you to remain in 'observer' mode, making associations and connections with your dream setting.

Dream themes

Not all settings will take us back to childhood haunts as Ian's did, though many people find themselves returning again and again in dreams to their childhood home, school, college, or university. These recurring settings help us to recognize current dream themes and to identify these same themes in waking experience. Although it isn't always immediately apparent, each dream gives us a window on a current theme. If we are taken back to some place or time in the past, it is usually because we have some 'unfinished business' there – like Ian – which leaves us carrying some unresolved trauma into similar waking situations in the present.

The setting of the dream may well give the strongest clue to where and when the troublesome pattern began. It also gives an opportunity to raise our consciousness around our behaviour in this environment. If you choose to work consciously with the situation, catching yourself in waking as you unconsciously repeat the pattern, you will find that your dream theme will start to change, until you no longer need to find yourself in that location and time of your life.

Journey settings

A common recurring theme is the journey dream. If you find yourself on a railway station, in the car, at a ferry terminal, or airport, the dream setting immediately speaks of a journey of some kind. The mode of travel indicated by the setting will usually relate to the nature of the journey you are making in your life right now. You may be 'letting the train take the strain', or the dream may be saying something about your life running on fixed tracks, always making scheduled stops.

The dream environment gives the context for the type of symbolic journey you are now making, and then there is the dynamic of how you are behaving and feeling within that setting. How well equipped and ready to make the journey are you? Can you find your platform, passport, or ticket? Do you find yourself forever packing your suitcase but never actually making the journey? Or do you get there too late, so that you 'miss the boat'? What might such dreams be saying about the way you conduct your life? How would it be if you could make changes to break this pattern? What would you need to help you to make such a change?

Embarrassing settings

Which of us hasn't had a bathroom dream at some time? The sort where you are desperate to find a toilet but however hard you search, there isn't one free. Or if there is, it has no door, leaving you with no privacy or dignity. Perhaps the toilet is really dirty, someone else's excrement – literally their 'shit' – making it impossible for you to use. Or you find yourself naked, trying frantically to hide from colleagues at work or people that you feel you need to impress.

Such insecurity dreams evoke great anxiety, giving lie to the confident, upfront image we may have carefully built for ourselves over the years. They may highlight a more vulnerable, less socially capable part of us, who lives in permanent anxiety beneath the veneer of sophistication. Questions about the balance we try to maintain between privacy and intimacy come in here too.

I remember once reading a newspaper article about a woman who was with the Special Forces in the army. On a most realistic and brutal training session she was 'kidnapped' and interrogated by a supposed enemy snatch force, in reality some members of another squad. During prolonged and frightening questioning she asked repeatedly to be allowed to go to the toilet. Her interrogators refused several times, so finally she chose to stand there and urinate while still clothed, in defiance. It takes a certain type of strength or desperation to be able to do this, but it is one way to cope! She heard later that the men questioning her had been most impressed with this rebellious act, seeing it as a sign of her strength and obduracy. Certainly she broke the 'victim' mould. I am not advocating this extreme example as a realistic alteration to your usual behaviour in waking, but in a dream, anything is possible!

Incongruent settings

Many dream settings reflect our social life. We may find ourselves at a party, in a bar or hotel, or perhaps at the beach with friends or family. These familiar settings may seem exactly as they are in waking, though sometimes something about the place will be different, even incongruent. These incongruent details are often the Dream Maker's ploy to get our attention. Here's a dream of this type:

'I am in a big, utilitarian warehouse with an older man. We each have clipboards and we're stocktaking. The warehouse is stacked with goods; it feels as if we've been doing this boring task for a long time and it could go on forever. I wander over to the loading bay, an opening in the wall on the first floor that leads to a platform with a rope and pulley, like the old mills used to have. Looking down into the yard below I see a big seesaw right under the platform. I can't resist it and jump out onto one end, then somersault over to the other end and back again. When I stop, I see that I'm dressed in a clown's costume!'

This dream speaks for itself, describing not a literal, but an emotional perception of the dreamer's work environment. The seesaw, incongruent in the workplace, draws the dreamer's attention to the way he 'plays the clown' to escape the more onerous aspects of his job. He 'seesaws' between responsibility and the need for fun in his life. It's important, of course, to find and hold this balance, but in appropriate ways.

Setting and symptoms

At times the dream environment can be so powerful a part of the inner process that the experience of it carries over into waking, producing a strong physical effect. A friend once rang and asked if she could come to see me as she wasn't feeling well, and felt there was some connection with a recent dream that was troubling her.

She arrived on my doorstep almost in a state of collapse. She was feverish, had a headache, a red rash over her face and neck, as well as being dizzy and terribly thirsty. She shared a dream where she had been stuck on a narrow ledge on a cliff in the desert for a long time in the hot sun. The path she had been following had petered out, there was a sheer drop before her, and she was in a state of panic, afraid to move.

She was so caught in the experience of this dream that withdrawing to observe the setting was out of the question, yet obviously the desert conditions could be contributing to her symptoms. We didn't need to revisit the dream, as she had never really left it on waking! To help ease her panic, I let her know that I was there to accompany her now, and invited her to look right and left, instead of staring down at the sheer drop before her. As she did this the panic began to ease: she spotted a little path, like an animal track, going down the cliff. She followed this to the bottom and was met by a man of the desert, the leader of a caravan of camels.

This scruffy, disreputable old man with a sly sense of humour seemed an unlikely dream helper. But he clearly knew his way around the desert landscape and let her join his caravan. He took her to an oasis where she could rest in the shade, drinking and bathing in the water before journeying on.

I took my cue from him and simply left her to rest. When she woke a couple of hours later, all her symptoms had disappeared. She felt refreshed, relaxed, and completely amazed at the transformation she had just experienced.

Many people panic when faced with a dream's symbolic picture of events in their life. It is a natural enough reaction to get 'hot and bothered' when we have to face the fact that we can't follow a particular path any further, that it has led us to the edge of a precipice, and it feels as if there is nowhere else to go. At such times we do need a little help from our friends, both inner and outer.

Such strong dreams come at a time of crisis in our lives, where unpalatable choices may need to be made. They are symbolically expressing a dilemma. The desert experience is heavily symbolic. Those seeking spiritual guidance or transformation journey there by choice. The scapegoat is cast into isolation there. But we can find ourselves caught unwittingly there, ill prepared, as my friend did.

The desert is a hostile, non-nurturing environment, extremely dangerous to those who do not know it well. We get burnt in the dry desert heat. Symbolically, my friend's denial and passivity regarding her current life situation was burnt away. It was a kind of ordeal by fire, potentially cleansing and healing, but in a landscape that demanded immense respect.

The deserts of the world are littered with the bones of people who have lost their way. When you are working alone with an extreme dream environment, be sure to call in your dream helpers before you begin. If you have symptoms of any kind, it is wiser to check them out with a doctor first, as well as working with the dream and the inner processes.

The elements in dream settings

The elements – fire, water, air, and earth – can all carry clear symbolic messages into our dreams. The fire of the desert describes a very different state of being from the warmth of the hearth or the fun of a bonfire. Watery dreams can be strongly affecting. The little stream babbling over stones is a world away from the raging torrent of the river in full spate, carrying everything before it. Water usually symbolizes the emotions and feelings, so the type of water in your dream images says a great deal. A swimming pool, dam, or canal suggests feelings that are contained in a man-made construction, something we have built for ourselves, or which has been artificially created for us. A tranquil pool in a forest clearing shows a more natural container. Even turbulent water or a whirlpool is still a force of nature, not something imposed upon the surroundings.

People who are afraid of their feelings may well be afraid of water, in dreams and in waking, avoiding it whenever they can. Those who prefer to skim the surface of their emotions may find themselves in a boat, perhaps bringing in the element of air to fill their sails. Others may be completely at home in the depths, swimming with dolphins, exploring a lake or the ocean bed.

Airy dreams include flying in any kind of flying machine, or those wonderful moments when we suddenly find that we can fly unaided. You may even experience yourself as a bird, swooping and soaring on the thermals. The view from up there can be fabulous, but connection with people and events down on the ground may become more remote.

There is a value in being able to rise above things, gaining a different, wider perspective. But we all have to come down to earth sooner or later. Dreams of falling are often one way of doing this. They can be frightening, but if you remember that this is a dream, you will not be physically hurt. Can you allow yourself to fall? The Senoi people would suggest this. Let yourself fall, and land, without fear. Then get up, dust yourself off, look around and see what you have fallen into! Some people who attempt this find that they can fly and choose where to land.

The dream of the beech wood mentioned earlier shows that the dreamer has a good connection with nature and the earth. But for some, the earth itself holds terrors. They may dream of being lost in a dark forest, or of being swallowed up by an earthquake, or buried alive. Too much earth can feel suffocating and claustrophobic to an airy type. When we look at earthy dreams we also look at being grounded, at making a secure connection with the environment and our body, of knowing our place on the earth, though for some the fear is of having 'feet of clay' or becoming a 'stick-in-the-mud'.

When you find yourself in an uncomfortable element in your dreams, just remember that you can experiment, trying out new ways of being in your dreamworld and calling on any helpers who may feel more at home in that environment. (You will see in chapter three how the elements relate to the four functions that Jung described.)

I could fill a whole book with dream examples where the setting is the starting point for deep and satisfying dreamwork, but your own experience will be the best teacher. The exercises that follow will get you started. Do them with several dreams, to help your emerging awareness of current dream themes.

Using dream exercises

You will be trying out many exercises as you work your way through this book and it is important that you go about doing them in the right way from the start.

Be aware that each dream is a powerful inner expression of some aspect of your life. It comes to you as a gift, created by a source of refined intelligence that has your best interests at heart. Give the dream the respect it deserves. Always set aside a time when you won't be interrupted to do an exercise. Turn down the volume on your phone. Create realistic limits to the time you will spend on this work.

Don't choose a nightmare or frightening dream when you first try a new exercise. Always be gentle with yourself. Begin by working with something that feels less threatening, working up to looking at the scarier ones. Remember that something within you is afraid and it would be brutal to rush this part of you into some terrifying work before you even know what the exercise is likely to produce. Having said that, even some apparently innocuous dreams can have a surprisingly powerful effect when we work with even the early exercises. All the more reason to take care...

Never rush into revisiting a dream before your observer has got some perspective on it. Make your associations first, too, as Ian did. This gives a necessary orientation before you start to move into deeper layers of dreamwork and altered states of consciousness. Some of the examples given in this chapter are of more advanced work. Please don't go back into the dream setting to change anything at this point. The aim of the exercises in this chapter is to gain a fuller experience of the setting, just as it is.

You will also be learning to hold your focus in a disciplined way and to begin to develop an astute observer. That's quite enough for now. If things spontaneously develop, that is fine, but don't start tampering with the dream just for the sake of it, or because it seems like a good idea at the time! Relax, stay open, and see what comes.

Dream-centred associations

In the Transformative Dreamwork approach when we speak of associations, we don't mean the Freudian psychological tradition of 'free association' where one association leads to another, and another, and another. If we were to do this, we could end up a long way away from the dream that we started with.

For example, using Ian's dream, he might have made the initial association with his grandmother's house and then gone into a chain of associated memories from his childhood. This is all very interesting perhaps, but where is their connection with the dream? When we find ourselves doing this it's a good idea to stop and ask, 'Where does this relate to what is actually in my dream?' and go back to the dream to reconnect with your focal point. In this case, the focus is on Ian's dream setting, a cobbled street on a dark evening. In the dream, his grandmother was nowhere to be seen. It was because the little boy was alone, cold, wet, and feeling left out that this dream put Ian in touch with his current situation and feelings. If there were something significant to be learned from his trips to the corner shop with his grandmother, you can be sure that both she and the shop would be in the dream!

By using the image of a daisy in the diagram opposite, you can see how, in dreamwork, we regard each association in the light of what is at the centre. We keep coming back to the dream, which anchors us and keeps the focus. After you have done part two of this exercise, you may want to go on to write your additional memories and other connections in your dream journal. We don't want to deny them, and they can undoubtedly give us a wider picture. They may even lead into some valuable and enjoyable creative writing. But the daisy structure keeps us to the purpose of the exercise, revealing something specific about the dream.

I have included Ian's daisy above as an example. In the following exercise you can create your own.

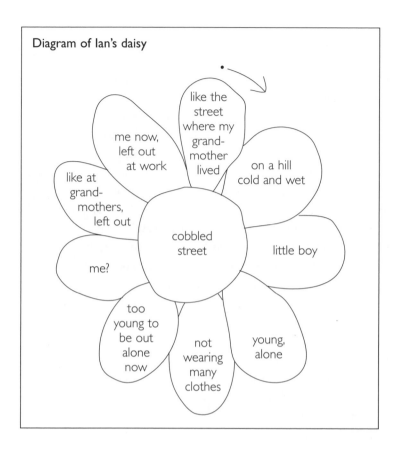

Diagram of Ian's daisy

- me now, left out at work
- like the street where my grand-mother lived
- on a hill cold and wet
- like at grand-mothers, left out
- cobbled street
- little boy
- me?
- too young to be out alone now
- not wearing many clothes
- young, alone

Exercise four: observing your dream setting

In this exercise we draw upon our inner observer, by viewing the dream as a film or play, as we did earlier in this chapter. The purpose of this is to disentangle you from emotional involvement for a while, so that you get a more detached, wider perspective from your place in the audience. In some dreams the setting changes several times. To begin with, stay with just the setting of the opening scene.

Part one

- Choose a dream from your journal and reread it to refresh your memory. Then let your attention go to the beginning of the dream. Take time to focus on the setting.

• Now ask: Where do you find yourself as the dream begins? Are you indoors or outdoors? Is this place familiar, or new to you? If it is familiar, are things just the same as they are in waking? Or do you recognize this setting from previous dreams? Is it perhaps a combination of both?

• If you find yourself in unknown surroundings, take a good look around to get the feel of the place. When you are ready, ask yourself: what is the purpose of such a place? What activity or event might happen here? Do you get a sense of the time of day or season of the year? What sort of mood does this setting create?

• Take a minute or two to consider what the setting seems to connect you with, and how you feel about it. Then, when you are ready, move on to part two of this exercise. Remember to stay with the dream setting, not allowing yourself to be drawn into a chain of free associations.

Part two

• Turn to a fresh page in your dream journal. In the centre, write the dream setting in one or two words, and draw a circle around it. This forms the centre of your flower. The associations are the petals. Ask yourself: where do you find yourself as this dream begins? What does this place mean to you? Write your answers and draw petals around them, connecting them with the centre.

• How does this setting relate to the settings in your waking life? Record your answer on another petal. How does this place feel? Again, put your answer in a petal. Keep moving around the flower, asking yourself questions related to the setting as it is in the dream, not in waking, and drawing petals around your answers. You will finish with a daisy-like flower shape.

Reflections on parts one and two

How easy or difficult did you find this exercise? Spend a moment or two looking at the nature of any problems you had. Were you able to hold the focus? Did you write what you found in your dream journal? Was there anything getting in the way?

Sometimes when we feel resistance to doing an exercise it's better to move the focus to the resistance itself, instead of trying to fight it. Put 'my resistance' or 'my block' in the centre of a daisy and allow the associations and feelings to come. Then, when you understand what is going on, you may find you can go back to the exercise – or not!

A dream with a vague setting won't lend itself well to this exercise. Occasionally there may be a dream that seems to have no setting at all, just riveting action or interchange. If your most recent dream is like this, then don't use it for this exercise. If you choose an unsuitable dream you may end up feeling a failure, needlessly. I usually suggest using the most recent dream, but if this is clearly unsuitable, choose another. Why not try opening your dream journal at random and working with the first dream you see?

Some of your answers may surprise you; they may connect you with places, people, or emotions that you haven't encountered for a long time. Don't be put off by this: it is the nature of dreamwork to yield surprises and deliver occasional shocks, bringing about greater self-awareness. You don't have to understand everything all at once!

Remember to take some time out for yourself afterwards. This also gives you time to digest what you have found before doing more. Later, after a break, you can do the final part of this exercise.

Part three

In this last part of the exercise we are going to revisit the dream to simply savour the setting. We will re-experience it as fully as possible, using all our senses, without taking any action or changing anything.

This work is full of paradox. When we let go of our search for meaning and surrender our ego to a full experience of the dream, suddenly the meaning is there! What now follows will move you into an altered state of consciousness by taking you back into the dream while fully awake, to enrich your experience of the setting.

At this level of dreamwork we need to be able to create a good, conscious container for the exercise. Place a time limit of ten minutes on your stay within the dream. You will be meeting your unconscious, and this may be a deeply seductive realm. The timescale is different here, and much can happen in very little time. Our aim is to maintain an edge of alert consciousness while keeping within the dream imagery. It gets easier with practice!

• Begin by bearing in mind all that you have learned from your observations and associations of the dream setting in parts one and two of this exercise.

• Sit quietly for a moment, and let those energies settle. Become aware of your breathing. Don't try to change it, just follow the gentle rhythm of your breath. Feel the breath moving softly in and out of your body and see if your energy can follow each in-breath, moving down from your head and into your belly. This will help to calm your mind and create a receptive inner space.

• Remembering your dream setting, see it now through your eyes in the dream, so that you once again become a part of that dream. This time take a good look around – really see this place you find yourself in. Give yourself time to take in as much as you can, noticing any sounds and smells too. Feel the ground beneath your feet, or the solidity and texture of whatever you may be sitting or lying on. Experience the quality of the air around your body, the temperature, and climate. Do you feel you have enough personal space around you? Is it clear or cluttered? Is this place in sympathy with the way you like to be, or do you find it uncomfortable? Be aware of the mood of this place, and of the effect it has upon you.

• When you are ready, become aware of your breathing once more, feeling the gentle movement in your body, so that you leave the exercise in the way that you came in. Coming back into the physical sensations of your body, open your eyes and look around, noticing details of the room, to help you return to full consciousness.

• Write up the experience as fully and flowingly as you can in your dream journal, along with any thoughts and feelings you may have about it all.

Reflections on part three

Were you able to go back into the dream and feel fully present there? Some people can do this with ease, while others need to persevere, using the exercise with several dreams until they become accustomed to this technique. Could you stay within the time limit? It's a discipline that becomes increasingly necessary as the work intensifies. We need to create a balance between holding on to our sense of purpose and surrendering to what the dream offers. I don't want you to be pulled off-centre by the 'other world' of the unconscious, just to get a taste of it and return fully to yourself.

You don't need to be afraid of reaching slightly altered states of consciousness; just stay mindful of the waking world. Having something to eat or drink – a hot cup of something or some fruit – might be a good way to end this piece of work. It will help to ground you in the present, and give you a quiet transition time to review what you have learned, before moving back into everyday conscious activity. Remind yourself that you can work with the dream environment again in the same way with other dreams. This will deepen and vary your experience of the variety that these exercises can offer.

three ~~3~~ *Who am I in the dream?*

three *3 Who am I in the dream?*

You may be surprised when you are asked to look at yourself in the dream. Most people will assume that, 'Well, in the dream, I'm me, aren't I, just myself?' The truth is not always that simple. First we have to look at what we mean by 'self'. In psychological terms, the self is usually taken to mean the ego. This centre of self-consciousness is our choice maker, determining how we behave, building our self-image and self-esteem, dictating how much of ourselves we allow other people to see and know. It is aware of our hopes and fears, the goals we set ourselves, and can be highly motivated towards the preservation of its point of view. We come to believe that this ego identity personifies all that we are. We interchange 'ego' with 'I'.

Yet what happens to this ego when we go to sleep at night? It disappears whenever we lose consciousness. Without it, something within us continues to exist, waking to the ego again the next morning. When you stop to think about it, this can be unsettling. It suggests that there is more to us than just the ego. The Italian psychologist Roberto Assagioli thought so, and developed the map opposite in an attempt to illustrate his view of the psychological constitution of the human being.

Although this map is two-dimensional it suggests something three-dimensional and full of movement. The circle of the field of lighted consciousness represents our everyday state of awareness. The small dot at the centre is the ego described above, while the whole of the egg represents our potential, of which we remain largely unaware. This graphic representation reminds us that we have so much more to draw upon in life than we realize – if we can free ourselves from experiencing life only from the ego perspective.

The broad band of the middle unconscious immediately surrounding the circle of awareness is where our various

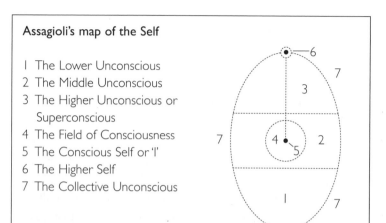

Assagioli's map of the Self

1 The Lower Unconscious
2 The Middle Unconscious
3 The Higher Unconscious or
   Superconscious
4 The Field of Consciousness
5 The Conscious Self or 'I'
6 The Higher Self
7 The Collective Unconscious

experiences are assimilated. All that we have ever known and learned is here. It is also the realm of mental and imaginative activity that shapes and develops our experiences. It could be called a place of gestation, facilitating the transition of experience before it comes into consciousness. The information stored here is easily available to us, accessible through the dotted lines of the field of lighted consciousness. You will have noticed that all of the lines in the diagram are broken. This permeability illustrates the capacity of information to move between one area and another, and the possibility of expansion.

The higher unconscious is associated with an ascent, the Masculine principle, and the light that can lead to illumination – the wonderful 'aha!' moment of recognition and insight, as when a brilliant shaft of sunshine breaks through on a cloudy day. Its energy is spiritual, inspirational, and intuitive, often found in the fields of creativity, philosophy, and science. It is a place of the higher feelings, altruistic love, moral ethics, and ecstasy. It culminates in the star at the top, which represents the higher Self, that is, true self-awareness and the mediator of the individual's experience of their god. (When referring to the higher Self, I use a capital S, to distinguish it from the ego's perception of self.) It is this true Self that, rising above ego-consciousness, maintains a constant presence throughout our life.

Some people are able to reach this place voluntarily, through spiritual practices such as prayer, meditation, and contemplation. But we cannot sustain the intensity of living as this Self, and tend to fall back into the self again. Occasionally, we will find ourselves involuntarily spirited up to the higher Self, in moments of creative inspiration and transcendence.

The higher unconscious can become a place of refuge in the desperate flight from physical suffering; during illness; sexual, physical, or emotional abuse; or at times of trauma, such as accident or attack. Usually we come back into the body when the danger or illness passes. However, prolonged abuse, or long-term illness that has a devastating physical and emotional effect can cause some people to want to remain 'in the light'. Such people may then appear to be 'high', spiritual, calm and wise. But their connection with the body becomes tenuous, lacking vitality, perhaps leaving the body vulnerable and weak, open to further illness. Ungrounded in this way we are also more likely to lose things, have accidents, be absent-minded, and perhaps not eat sensibly. As human beings, we need to inhabit the body fully, developing a healthy balance between spirit and matter.

A more conscious rejection of the body occurs in some religions, where spiritual devotion, such as that of the mystic nuns and monks of the Middle Ages, requires the subjugation of the body and ego to the spirit.

Assagioli described the lower unconscious as containing the psychological activities that direct the life of the body: fundamental drives and primitive urges, many complexes charged with intense emotion and phobias, obsessions, compulsive urges, and paranoid delusions. I have come to understand this as a place of shadowy, forgotten, and unknown things. Here we encounter the theme of descent again, to the archetypal Feminine, the dark, an often sorrowing and painful journey. It is a frightening place, but if we try to cut off from it, sooner or later illness, accident, loss, or despair will pull us down. Depression may imprison us here, too. Yet visit it we must, for it is here that we find great healing and ancient wisdom. This path also brings us to our god, by a slower, very different but equally honourable route, the 'night sea journey'. This is soul-making work, and I feel sure that if Assagioli were creating this map today he would recognize the value of this journey and place a star there, too.

We are all strongly influenced by the collective unconscious that surrounds the egg. This is everything that is 'not I'. It contains our cultural heritage, from that of our immediate community to all the peoples of the earth. The accumulated knowledge of our ancestors, from our earliest beginnings, resides here. Jung described this as 'The two million-year-old man' that is in all of us. (from *CG Jung Speaking*). This is the home of the archetypes, which we will look at again in chapter six.

The outer line of the diagram does not divide us from the collective unconscious but sets a limit upon the Self. We constantly process information from the collective unconscious and our thoughts and actions go out into it, creating an effect, and making a personal contribution. Years ago I had a dream that goes some way towards illustrating this: *'I am on a hotel balcony, somewhere in South Africa, I think. It is warm and sunny and I am looking out over a landscape of reddish sand dunes – mile upon mile of them. I marvel at the way they are constantly reshaped by the movement of the wind, a process that has gone on since the planet was created.*

'Suddenly I find myself kneeling among the dunes. I crouch close to the sand and blow, gently. To my delight, a small wave of sand forms, adding my personal contribution to the overall pattern. This gives me a warm sense of the rightness of all things, and my ability to make a difference in the moment, fully accepting that, in time, it will be obliterated by the wind.'

Our dreams draw frequently upon familiar material from the collective unconscious. Sometimes we'll say, 'I know why I dreamt that! It's because of the programme I watched on television last night.' That may well be so, but it is only a starting point. There will be layers of meaning attached to the contents of that programme, but also to its connection with your dream, and its relevance to your life.

When we witness, via the media, terrible disasters happening in some distant part of the world or closer to home, our dreams may become disturbed for a while as we make an unconscious connection with the surge of grief moving through the collective. Such events not only resonate with similar personal experiences, but also dig deep into the race memories and sensibilities of humankind. The unexpected public outpouring of grief at the untimely death of Diana, Princess of Wales, demonstrated this dynamic in action.

Through this psychic interaction with the collective unconscious, we find that we are not isolated and alone as human beings, even though at times we may feel so. Fairy tales, with minor variations, are the same throughout the world, drawing, as they do, on the experiences stored in the collective unconscious. A writer, painter, or composer may create something and be told it's very similar to someone else's work, yet cannot consciously remember ever having read, seen, or even heard of that particular piece of work before. Accusations of plagiarism sometimes arise through people drawing on the contents of the collective unconscious in this way.

Have you ever found yourself humming a tune, when the person you are with says, 'I was just thinking of that song. It's been in my head all morning.' How porous is the boundary between the self and the collective!

Assagioli's diagram attempts to illustrate more of our whole being. The psyche, or soul, can move through all the areas of this map with grace and ease, speaking to us in dreams of its discoveries and pointing out things that we need to become aware of. When this information comes in to our consciousness as we wake, we must take care that it does not become diluted or distorted by a defensive ego.

Resistance to dreamwork

The defensive ego

We all have an inner censor of some kind, affecting many areas of our lives, not just our dream recall. For some of us, it is a defensive ego with fixed ideas about acceptable behaviour or standards. A healthy ego, on the other hand, will be a good decision maker, choosing constantly what is or isn't appropriate, knowing when to risk a little, and when to say no.

These choices are based upon layers of experience, accumulated over the years, and the lessons learned from previous successes and mistakes. Sometimes, though, the ego can have too narrow a field of vision, limiting our potential life experience by an over-stringent selection of what is or is not personally or socially acceptable.

A person who may have suffered rejection as a child, or been severely judged or criticized, will not have been encouraged to trust their own judgement and develop a healthy ego. Very strict parents, caught within their own narrow limitations, may have communicated their fears and inhibitions to their children, who grow up considering them to be their own. This type of ego, while it keeps you protected, is not open to new experiences and does not like to be challenged.

A defensive ego will take some time to be convinced by the other parts of you that now want to move forward and grow. It may hold a negative opinion about dreamwork, and may undermine your efforts, causing you to doubt that you have made a wise choice, or that you are capable of doing the work, if it allows you to recall your dreams at all. Even a healthy ego may feel that the concept of respecting the dream, listening to what it has to say, and being guided by it within our waking lives can threaten its own autonomy, or usurp its position at the helm, and menace its sense of security.

The defender and the censor

If the wounds of childhood run deep and we did not usually receive the support we needed, we will have learned to cope alone. We retreat from pain, which once felt too much to bear, and defend ourselves in any way we can, so that we will never have to experience that pain again. Some of us learn to evade pain very successfully, keeping ourselves safe from attack, criticism, fear, and humiliation. We unconsciously build a defender who serves us well, and who is always on the lookout, always there for us. This defender will be slow to trust and may be deeply suspicious of new people, situations, and ideas. It lives within the unconscious as a sub-personality, literally an aspect of our personality that is beneath our conscious awareness. We may not realize the part it plays in our everyday life, or know that it exists at all. Dreamwork will represent the unknown to the defender, and many of us are afraid of the unknown. Who knows what our dreams may bring? The duty of the defender is to keep such untried and untested ideas at bay. It experiences them as possible threats, and is unable to see the opportunities they truly represent. It will have served you well in childhood, but may not recognize that you are now an adult, less vulnerable, and capable of making better-informed decisions.

The censor tends to be based primarily on people or role models taken from outer life. A dream figure that appears to uphold the law or morality will often represent our own censor. On our workshops and courses, we often encounter such dream figures, for example: policeman, commander, director, bullying boss, disapproving parent, critic, or judge.

In contrast, the defender inhabits a deeper level of the unconscious, and may take almost any form, setting up a powerful resistance to change. A fierce animal, a knight or warrior, a locked door, a brick wall, a barbed wire fence, a hostile army, or a huge block of ice are common symbolic images for this often formidable part of ourselves. Both operate autonomously.

The censor may reduce us to the position of powerless child, unable to trust our own instincts and our own choices. The defender, on the other hand, will often give a knee-jerk response, either trying to remove us from any perceived threatening situation, or ruthlessly demolishing the opposition. Occasionally the defender will choose not to reveal itself and will instead offer an image of what it is defending. This can be anything from a small frightened child, a wounded animal, or a sick person, to a fragile vase or container, our family home, or even a castle.

Exercise five: meeting resistance

• If you find you are not remembering your dreams, pause for a moment now, close your eyes, and try to let go of the examples we've given above. Invite in the particular character or obstacle that is keeping you from your dream life. You may receive an image or thought very quickly, or you may find this takes some time. Try not to dismiss or reject whatever comes (this may be the censor at work).

• Stay with the image, accept it, and consider how you feel about this portrayal of what blocks you: is there some sense of shame or denial, or pride that says, 'That's nothing to do with me!' Can you feel a leap of recognition? Does this image make sense, set in the context of your life?

• Write up all of this in your journal, including any connections and associations that you may be making.

At least now you know the opposition! You don't have to take any further action at this point. Just being aware of the vitality of this aspect of yourself can be enough to bring about a spontaneous change in your relationship with your dreams. This exercise in discrimination helps to build a detached but compassionate observer that can support the defensive ego. From this position, we can be more tolerant, willing to consider another point of view, and less attached to outcomes or results.

The inner editor

You may have noticed that the defensive ego edits the dream as you record it, reorganizing the sequences to make sense, and omitting or changing whatever it considers distasteful. It will also make judgements about your dreams, often deciding that the short, seemingly boring ones aren't worth recording at all!

In your work so far, it is probably your ego that has selected the dreams to write and work with. From now on, resolve to work with your next remembered dream, whatever its content. Try repeating one of the previous exercises with a short dream that you have simply ignored. You will find that such dreams can yield great rewards when given a little attention.

Exercise six: discovering your dream self

Before you start, remember there's no right or wrong in dreamwork. If you're happy with the way you are in the dream, that's fine. If not, your dreams will help you to explore other ways of being.

The dream self and waking self

• Begin the exercise by rereading your most recent dream to connect with it again.

• Consider how the dream affects you. What sort of feelings does it leave you with? Can you make any associations with your waking life by looking briefly at the setting, events, or characters in the dream?

• Staying with the idea from the previous chapter of seeing your dream as a movie or play, imagine that you are in the audience again, watching the performance. This time, pay particular attention to the 'you' in the dream, your dream self. We are not always quite who we think we are in dreams. Because of this waking ego expectation, we tend not to pay much attention to ourselves. Try to really focus upon this dream self now.

Connecting with yourself in the dream

• Are you able to hold your place in the audience and also see yourself as a character in the dream? Are you more drawn into being the dream 'you', experiencing the dream from this other identity? Perhaps you don't get a strong sense of yourself in the dream at all? It may be that you don't feel present or embodied, but find yourself observing what happens in the dream.

Your appearance

• Keeping the focus on your dream self, take a look at your clothes. Is what you are wearing suitable for the dream setting and activities? The following dream came shortly after a woman called Ann and her husband had moved from their flat in the town to a country cottage.

'I am walking across a ploughed field. It's pouring with rain, pelting down, and the earth is just thick mud. I'm cold and soaking wet. I hate it. The rain is ruining my favourite smart city suit and my high heels keep sinking into the mud. I feel thoroughly miserable and want to go home.'

This clear example of incongruent clothing shows Ann's resentment of this move, which had been instigated by her husband. She had reluctantly agreed because he was so enthusiastic, but recognized now that she was emotionally ill-prepared for this change of home environment and lifestyle.

Ann saw that she would continue to feel miserable if she tried to preserve her old 'townie' image, recognizing that a change of attitude was required, not just a change of clothes! She went out and bought a good weatherproof coat and boots, but also involved herself in the local community. Here she learned the old country ways from people who'd always lived there. Ann found that she was not just learning a great deal but having fun too. She loves her country life now, but has still kept her town connections, so that that part of her is also nurtured.

Your clothing

• Returning to your own dream, are your clothes those you normally wear? Do they remind you of an earlier time in your life? If you can't see your clothes clearly, take a look at your feet. When dreamworkers do this they sometimes find themselves wearing school shoes, or children's sandals. It can be startling to realize you are not the adult you thought you were in a dream. But it may explain why you aren't coping as well as you'd expect, or struggling to make sense of events. For most of us, there are times when we are unaware that our inner child has taken over. At such times we behave in a childlike or childish manner, inappropriate to the situation. If this is happening in your dreams it is also happening in waking and your Dream Maker wants you to become aware of it.

Being younger in a dream

A dream of being a different age takes us back in time, not always to childhood, but to any stage of our lives. It comes to show that we have 'unfinished business' from that period, which continues to affect us. We must take care not to blame the anxious child or rebellious teenager for displacing the ego sometimes. The inner child doesn't choose to do this, but is being evoked by current situations or relationships that trigger unresolved feelings from the past. Try to hold in mind a benign intent to 'recognize, accept, and befriend' what you find in your dreams, even if at first you feel embarrassed or angry.

• If you find that you are younger in the dream you are working on now, take a little time to reflect on how your life was then. How do you know you were that age in the dream? What was happening to you? How did you respond? How much choice did you feel you had?

Is something similar now being repeated in some way in your waking life? Do you have greater choices and support now?

Being naked in a dream

Many people dream of being naked at some time or another. If this feels appropriate, as in an erotic or sexual dream, allowing you to enjoy a fuller experience of your sensuality, then that is fine. But if you are in a public place and feel embarrassed or ashamed of your nudity, what might the dream be saying? Is it speaking of your vulnerability in some way? When we are naked before another, all pretence is gone and self-esteem issues can be stirred up.

• Look at the context of your dream. Where do you find yourself compromised? If the dream setting is the workplace, is the dream saying something about your feelings of inadequacy at work? Many people with responsible jobs have the thought, 'If they knew what I was really like, I'd get the sack'. They live from day to day waiting to be found out. If you are in a hotel, at an award ceremony, visiting a club or at a party, does your insecurity lie in social settings?

• Look at how you cope in such dreams. Is there anyone around to support you? How much support do you have in your waking life? Remember you can call upon a dream helper whenever you need to.

Your behaviour in the dream

Our dreams don't always move back through earlier stages of our lives to show us aspects of ourselves. The dream self may look just as you do now, yet they might behave differently. The person who is shy in waking may become an outrageous flirt, for instance, in a dream setting. Someone usually fair-minded may behave totally unreasonably. An honest, upright person may bend the rules or break the law, without conscience.

These dreams come to attempt to restore balance. They show us where we are in danger of becoming fixed in our attitudes and habits, and shock us into awareness of the strength of our inner critic by showing us the polarized opposite of our usual behaviour. This may well be part of the make-up of our personality. It might be something we have a natural, though repressed, tendency towards. Everyone has a darker, shadow side that the waking ego chooses to deny. We all have a fun-loving, lighthearted aspect, which a critical ego may dismiss as unworthy, causing us to become overly serious or too heavily work orientated – or vice versa! Again, see if you can find the wisdom and compassion to tolerate these less welcome aspects of yourself. You don't have to be perfect – no one is!

• Now let's see how you are behaving in the dream. Do you have the leading role or a smaller part? In this role, are you active, involved, and aware of what is going on? Or are you an observer, taking no real part? Are you calling the shots or is someone else in charge? How do you feel about your role and your degree of involvement?

• Write your findings in your journal, then compare this dream self with how you are in waking. Which do you prefer? Are there more similarities or contrasts between your dream self and your waking self? Do you ever behave the way this dream self behaves? If so, in what circumstances? Is there something you can take from the dream to use in your daily life?

The four functions

Taking on board the insights you have gained from this exercise, let's now look at Jung's description of the four functions, or types of behaviour. Jung recognized that we are all predisposed towards certain types of behaviour, or more accurately, ways of receiving and expressing experience. He identified four predominant types (see page 63). Only one of these four will be your preferred or superior function. Most of us also have a secondary function that we are reasonably at home with, usually one of those on either side of our superior function. The one we will have most trouble with is the one opposite, our weakest or inferior function.

For example, people who are primarily thinking types will have confidence in expressing themselves in words. They will tend to be most receptive to new information through the mind. This person may be able to think intuitively, or to be very organized in their approach to life, relying on the sensation function. The weakest function, the one that will cause them most difficulty, is the polarized, feeling function, which involves the emotions. Anyone with an over-clinical mind may lack compassionate rapport in relationships. Thinkers are especially susceptible to becoming unsettled in unsuitable relationships because, when their emotions enter, the mind flies out of the window!

When you can identify your preferred function you will probably recognize that you can fairly easily access those either side of it on the map. For instance a natural intuitive type may also be a very feeling person, or be able to think intuitively, as some scientists and many artists do, but they will probably tend to be rather clumsy or have a poor sense of direction, or are always misplacing things because of their weak sensation function. The absent-minded professor who searches for ages for his spectacles, not realizing they are on his head is a good example of this!

Each function has its own pace, too. Intuition, associated with the element of fire, is the fastest, where we can see the whole concept in a blinding flash. Next comes thinking, linked with air. Those we call 'head types' can also be very speedy in thought, action, and speech. Feeling, the watery element, comes next, as there is a flow to the feeling process that takes time. To Jung, the true feeling function was one of valuing, concerned with the relative worth of our experiences. The emotions are a kind of by-product of this valuing process. Finally, the sensation function, that of earth, is the slowest. People of this type are practical, down to earth, capable, and reliable, and will need concrete evidence of anything new. For a sensation type, only seeing is believing!

Does any of this strike a chord with you, either in waking or in dream life? What might your strongest function be? Which do you find most difficult, in yourself and others? Next is an exercise that may help you to be clearer.

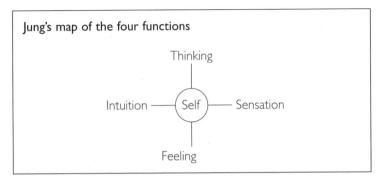

Jung's map of the four functions

Thinking

Intuition —(Self)— Sensation

Feeling

Exercise seven: colouring your functions

• Open your dream journal at random. Using the dream on that page, take a coloured pen or pencil and highlight all the feelings or emotions of the dream. You may, for instance, have written that you are worried, anxious, or tearful. Or perhaps there was excitement, love, tenderness, and laughter? Be sure to include every emotion.

• How much colour is there on the page when you've finished? Rereading the dream, do you find you were experiencing more emotionally than you have actually written?

• Now rewrite the dream, this time putting in everything you felt. If you have written that you were upset for instance, try explaining more clearly just how you feel when you are upset. Then highlight this new, fuller version and compare the two. Isn't it interesting how, without realizing it, we take our feelings for granted? See how much richer the dream is when you write in this way! If your two versions of the dream are almost identical, it could be that the feeling function is not your strongest.

In any case, it would be good to do this exercise again. Use your description of yourself in a dream, or your description of your dream surroundings, and choose a different colour to highlight what you find, which will be to do with your experience of the sensation function. Then review it once again, looking for your thoughts and state of mind. (You could use the same dream each time, or separate ones.) Viewed together, these three may give some clues as to which function – feeling, sensation, or thinking – you favour and which you could develop more. Using this exercise with several dreams, or just keeping an awareness of it every time you write out a dream, will gradually help to make the picture clearer.

Because the intuition is so fleeting and elusive, it is not practical to use this exercise to try to recognize it. Déjà vu dreams, or ones where you sense something going on that is not explicit but later proves to be true, may hint at the intuition at work.

Try not to judge yourself. Our society may place greater value on thinking – educating us away from our natural inclinations and into striving for academic success. But in reality, all functions are equal and deserve respect. The differences between us add spice to life. So if you find your dream self functioning differently from your usual waking mode, perhaps the Dream Maker is offering a glimpse of how you were meant to be, or showing what you might need to restore balance to some area of your life.

Through the exercises in this book, we will encourage you to try out new approaches to the dream, favouring one function or another. Working with a dream in this way provides a kind of safety net, before we try out something similar in outer situations. In this chapter we have begun to differentiate between waking self or ego, the dream self, and the higher, or spiritual, Self. Each dream gives us the opportunity to regard each of these aspects of ourselves in some depth, and to choose what we need to integrate as we move towards growth and harmony.

If you look at several dreams in this way over a period of time, you will catch yourself repeating old patterns, limiting your creative potential to make choices from a position of greater awareness and discrimination. In waking situations too, you may find yourself running on automatic pilot at times, sleepwalking through life. If you begin to monitor yourself in dreams and in waking, you will recognize these developing patterns and catch yourself while repeating them. It takes some determination and time, but you'll gradually get there.

Improved relationships are one of the positive outcomes of this work, as you'll find you can spot the trap before you walk into it, and come up with a more original, creative response instead of the old emotional reaction. The anonymous poem below beautifully illustrates this learning curve:

From the Source, an autobiography in five chapters

CHAPTER ONE
I walk down the street
There is a deep hole in the sidewalk
I fall in.
I am lost
I am helpless
It isn't my fault
It takes forever to find a way out.

CHAPTER TWO
I walk down the same street
There is a deep hole in the sidewalk
I pretend I don't see it
I fall in again.
I can't believe I am in the same place
But it isn't my fault
It still takes a long time to get out.

CHAPTER THREE
I walk down the same street
There is a deep hole in the sidewalk
I see it is there
I fall in.
It's a habit
But my eyes are open
I know where I am
It's my fault
I get out immediately.

CHAPTER FOUR
I walk down the same street
There is a deep hole in the sidewalk
I walk around it.

CHAPTER FIVE
I walk down a different street.

We can learn so much about ourselves through this work! We all have the potential for change and growth, even if at first a part of us will deny it. The following exercise, the final one in this chapter, introduces another way of experiencing your dream self.

Exercise eight: embodying the dream self

• Take your journal and find a quiet room with a full-length mirror. Embody the dream self by standing before the mirror and closing your eyes. Remember how you are in a particular dream. Let your body sense the sheer physicality of the dream self.

• With your eyes still closed, take up the posture you hold at a key point in the dream. Hold this posture, really letting yourself feel it. Mimic the facial expression too. Make sounds or words, if appropriate, that reflect the personality of your dream self.

• What feelings, emotions, or sensations arise when you embody this other version of yourself? Are they familiar to your waking self?

• Open your eyes and look in the mirror. Do you ever look like this in waking? Are you surprised by what you see and feel? Is it very different from the way you normally experience yourself?

• Make a journal entry describing the experience.

Reflections on chapter three

Some of your experiences may have surprised, excited, or unnerved you, as you worked through them in this chapter. This stage can also be quite challenging work, as it is where our boundaries begin to become blurred and stretched.

If you have found some younger or different aspect of yourself in the dream, try to see it as the beginning of a new relationship. It is by building more secure and meaningful relationships with ourselves, through such work, that we are better able to relate to others. If painful feelings have been evoked, give them time and space to be, and honour them for they need to be expressed. Recognizing them can be part of your healing. Remember that they are not the whole of you, simply something that is moving through you that needs to run its course.

As Jung said, 'Becoming conscious is exhausting'! You may feel weary or drained after doing some of these deeper exercises with your dreams. Take care of yourself, giving yourself time to rest and relax, or change your energy by doing something different, but gentle to refresh yourself. Remind yourself to take a little extra time out if possible. Nurturing yourself in this way is all part of the journey.

Don't talk to others too much or too soon about what you find in these exercises. Give yourself time to digest things first. If someone else knows that you are trying to change some aspects of your behaviour, you may be put under pressure as you try to please, or to keep your word. Hold your vision for yourself if you can, and see if anyone notices the changes – don't expect too much immediately.

Don't rush into making life-changing decisions because of what you learn from an exercise or dream. Give it time. Contemplate the repercussions and feelings that may be evoked. Ask yourself, 'Is any part of me feeling uncomfortable about this choice?' If so, spend some time being with it, letting it have a voice. How familiar is this voice to you? How do you usually respond to what it has to say? Can you really accept its point of view? Wait and watch for a few more dreams. If you are on the right track, the message will become clear, and you can use the time in between to prepare yourself for the next step.

Take note of your next few dreams, as they will almost certainly add to what you have already discovered. We tend to dream in themes over a period of weeks or even months. All the dreams in one night will involve the same central theme. Each dream is a new window on an old problem, and each may offer a new solution.

four 4 Dreaming of people

What sort of people do you meet each night in your dreams? For most of us a large proportion of our dreams do contain other people. It is relatively rare in my experience for someone to have dream after dream where there is not another living soul. Working with such dreams we find that there were often one or two dream figures present, but they were not clearly defined, held no vitality, and so the dreamer discounted them.

When people with such dreams come into dreamwork their dreams gradually change. They become more relational, firstly with themselves, through the interaction with their dream self, then later with others in their dreams who benefit from this attention and take on more energy and clarity. This dreamwork experience enables them to practise interacting with others before they gradually move into more ease with social skills in waking situations.

The figures in our dreams bring us into awareness of relationships of all kinds. They may be people we know in waking, or public figures and celebrities we know of through the media but haven't actually met. Soap opera stars, who can take the place of the extended family for regular viewers, often have leading roles in our dreams, too. Then there are the dream characters, who don't resemble anyone in our waking experience but have a life of their own in the dreamworld. Some may be familiar, having appeared in many dreams, others may only be there once; while some may just be vague and shadowy figures in the background, or identifiable stereotyped groups of people rather than individuals.

Another common feature is the composite character who may be made up of elements of more than one person that we know in waking or in our dream life. This person is like someone we know, yet not quite the same. He or she behaves in ways this person wouldn't, or carries different attributes. We need to observe the variations in the behaviour and attitudes of composite characters. In this way we come to understand the qualities they bring, overlaying those of the original individual with something new and 'other'.

Dream characters

The amount or quality of energy these dream figures carry, coupled with the strength of our emotional response to them, will show their significance to our life process. But who are they, these people who can come into our dreams with such ease? What do they represent? There is a school of thought in dreamwork that says that everything and everyone in a dream is really 'I', the dreamer. This refers to a symbolic aspect, of course, and may be true, though it feels rather absolute to me. Dreams also speak to us of others, especially those we care about, those we are in awe of, and those of whom we are afraid. In short, our dreams are filled with those who share our lives.

We may say that dream characters hold a mirror for us, and show how we relate to different types of people in differing situations. They can highlight our attitudes and prejudices, and catch us as we act unthinkingly or without compassion. They are skilled at showing us the masks we wear and giving us role models we can learn from. The characters that frighten us remind us of our fears and inadequacies, giving us an opportunity to deal with, rather than deny, them.

Dreamwork requires us to examine our behaviour in relationship to our dream characters, and compare this with our behaviour in similar, waking, situations. We may be surprised by what we see! Getting to know our dream figures in this way helps us, in turn, to learn more about ourselves.

We may be much less guarded in a dream; capable of expressing thoughts and feelings we wouldn't normally show in waking. Or we may find our usual behaviour amplified in our exchanges with dream characters, so that we can become more aware of it and perhaps question how well it serves us. In working with the people in our dreams we find that we need to look not only at them, but also at ourselves.

As with everything else in a dream, the characters come to

contribute something to a current theme in our lives. Sometimes the roots of this theme may be in the past and the characters themselves either will be people we've known or will remind us of someone else. Even a dream set in our present life situation can lead us back to earlier experiences by association. Some simply give a very clear message, 'Look, this is how you are behaving. How do you feel about it? Are you going to do anything about it?'

Here is an example of such a dream. Clive, the dreamer, is in his forties. He is an experienced dreamworker who trained with me, and now assists on workshops and courses.

'I'm in my bath, lying back in the warm water relaxing, when the door opens and a man walks in! He comes over to the bath and starts to pour something in from a small bottle he's carrying. I'm furious and yell at him to get out!'

Clive woke, indignant still, at this unwelcome intrusion. The bathroom as the dream setting suggests privacy or intimate relationship. Yet this man in the dream was unknown to him. Clive immediately saw that the dream was another in the recurring theme of invasion of his personal space, which he had already worked with. He felt completely justified in his anger towards the dream figure.

But dreams don't come to tell us what we already know, and this situation of intrusion followed by an angry response was too familiar. Then Clive realized that the man hadn't spoken at all. He hadn't really been given a chance! In the dream Clive had seen him as interfering and spoiling his bath. He didn't even know what he had poured into the water. Curious now, Clive chose to return to the dream and question the intruder.

Instead of yelling at him the minute he walked in, Clive asked the man what gave him the right to intrude, and what he was doing there. The man looked surprised, saying:

'"Well, you did leave the door open. I meant well. I knew you needed to relax and I have some lovely bath oil that I thought I'd like to share with you, so that you'd enjoy your bath even more. I didn't realize you'd be offended. I'm sorry."'

This left Clive feeling a little deflated! He had always perceived invasion of his space as negative and harmful. Yet here was a helpful, well-intentioned, humble man! Clive conceded that he had indeed left the bathroom door unlocked, but suggested that the man might knock next time.

By now Clive was paying more attention to his habitual angry response than to the apparent invasion. If this is a theme for us, there will always be people in dreams and waking who will invade our space. But do we always have to get angry about it and shout at them without giving them a chance to reply?

The dream says that Clive leaves the door open for intruders to enter, so here is something he might go on to look at. Some people might take the unlocked door as an invitation to enter. It might signify more to them in the way of intimacy than we intend – some people just aren't very aware of boundaries anyway. You know the sort of people who interrupt, stand too close, and demand your attention for too long? We have to be responsible for setting and maintaining our own boundaries.

Possibly there is another dimension to this dream. What if the man is illustrating some opposite aspect of Clive's own behaviour that he is unaware of? Could the dream be showing that Clive himself is capable of thoughtlessly intruding on someone else's space when he feels he has something to offer? This concept may be difficult to take on board, but often what we accuse others of is something we are blind to in ourselves. The waking ego might say, 'Of course not! I would never invade someone else's space like that'. Note the terminology. 'Invade someone's space' is the ego's notion of what the man did. If the dream man does not have a problem with boundaries, or has an easy attitude to a level of intimacy that Clive seems to find threatening, is it actually such an invasion? As we said in chapter three, the ego is not the whole of us, and can be unnecessarily defensive. What if the man in Clive's dream represents a sub-personality, an aspect of our personality that we are unaware, or only fleetingly aware of, which lives in the subconscious? This puts a different angle on the dream, for it now seems to be showing Clive in relationship with some unconscious aspect of himself.

Clive tells me that, after spending quite some time dealing with his ego-resistance, he eventually came to recognize this dream character as carrying more of his 'essence' than the Clive-figure in the dream. So the dream self was less representative of the true Self than the dream character was! The man's behaviour, which appeared negative, was now appreciated as positive, along with his easy, helpful manner and caring attitude. Clive had recognized that in his dream he was caught up in a sub-personality, but this defensive 'Clive' in the bath was not truly representative of Clive himself. It was in fact a sub-personality that had temporarily taken over the ego position.

Needless to say, this is an advanced piece of dreamwork. It takes time and persistence to fully integrate such a different character and let go of the fixed ego perspective and our unconscious projections.

Projection and transference

When we fail to recognize and accept an unconscious part of ourselves, we will tend to 'put it out' onto others. The original configuration in Clive's dream shows how he was caught in unconsciously putting out something he interpreted as negative behaviour onto the dream figure. This is projection in psychological terms. What we project we also attract.

Have you ever wondered why you seem to attract a certain type of person in most of your relationships? A huge unconscious process may be at work here. One way to describe it is that on meeting someone new, we instantly sense that they have a capacity to behave in a certain way, and that they are suitable to take on a role in an ongoing unresolved dynamic in our lives. We don't perceive this consciously through the ego, but unconsciously, on a deeper instinctual level. Indeed, often the ego sees quite the opposite: the mild-mannered man who, some way into the relationship, becomes inexplicably jealous and controlling, or the warm, loving woman who withdraws her affection, becoming cold and aloof.

You will see that the projections become negative, because it is mostly these aspects of our own personality that we deny and project onto others. We transfer our bad feelings around 'unfinished business' with our parents or previous partners onto someone else and expect them to behave in the same way. If the instinct that drew us to them in the first place was right, they will usually oblige, sooner or later. This is called negative projection and transference.

On the other hand, people with very low self-esteem seem to live caught in a self-perpetuating negative view of themselves, projecting out all their positive qualities onto others. These people will readily tell you how wise, special, or beautiful you are, misplacing onto you some of their own unacknowledged wisdom or beauty. It is a seductive positive projection but is no more real than its counterpart, and may cause you to have an inflated opinion of yourself if you accept it unquestioningly.

With positive transference we almost always expect too much. We tend to see an ideal and not the human being with faults and weaknesses. Then we feel disappointed, betrayed, and angry when this person cannot live up to our expectations. At this point the transference turns around, becoming negative and destructive, which means that the relationship may not survive. Then, unless we become aware of what we are co-creating, we start the whole merry-go-round again with someone else.

Many subtleties and complexities colour the process of projection and transference of our feelings. Be aware of these possibilities as you work with your dreams. For now, let's take a closer look at sub-personalities, which can carry these unrecognized traits of our character into our dreams.

The role of sub-personalities

The term sub-personality implies something that lies beneath conscious perception. It does not imply inferiority. It suggests forgotten, hidden, or unknown aspects of our character that dwell at a level below our everyday conscious awareness.

We all have several highly individual sub-personalities. It is usually the ego that denies them, whether they are good and bad, so limiting our sense of who we are, hindering our emotional development and potential. This process is supported by one or more of the sub-personalities themselves, such as our personal defender, censor, critic, or judge. This type of sub-personality usually begins to manifest early, perhaps in infancy, to protect the child you were then. Unless challenged, it continues to perceive you as still being that child and tries to keep you in that child mode all your life.

The aspects of your personality that you deny and disown do not go away. They live on, gathering energy in your unconscious. At times they can leap up and grab you unawares, spilling over, causing you to react emotionally or out of character when triggered by somebody else's behaviour. This can be very damaging to our relationships and, ironically, to the ego's cherished self-image.

Of course, not all sub-personalities are negative, as we saw from Clive's dream. At times it is the fearful defended ego that perceives threats where there ·are none. Many of our sub-personalities are supportive and helpful when we begin to get to know them. Appearing as characters in our dreams, they can show us ways to break free from the constraints of the waking ego and reveal some of our unlived talents and abilities. Taking us beyond the limitations placed upon us by our family or culture, they can open us up to the discovery of our true self.

Recognizing sub-personalities

In waking and in dreams, many of the people we have relationships with may carry some aspect of a sub-personality. Our parents gave us the bare bones of our first sub-personalities, showing us by word and deed, how to behave as parents. The parent of the opposite gender also gave us our first experience of the 'other', the seeding of our understanding of how it is to be 'man' or 'woman'. This pool of knowledge was added to as our brothers and sisters demonstrated their way of being. The friends, enemies, and teachers we met at school, and employers and work colleagues contributed too. Partners and lovers will have played their part. Even chance encounters can be highly significant in giving us insight into a wider experience, a diversity in the myriad ways of the personality.

When any one of these people we currently have, or have

previously had, a relationship with appears in our dreams, they may be communicating something of what they unwittingly taught us about their personality and our own:

• They may be drawing your attention to someone currently in your life who is behaving in the same way, giving you an opportunity to consider whether or not it is appropriate. Is it what you want in your relationships now?

• They may be present in a compensatory way, to remind you of what you valued once but may not be getting enough of at present, or of your yearning for something you never had.

• Perhaps they have come to wake us up to our own behaviour in response to them. Supposing you meet your mother or father in a dream. Do you still react in the way you did when you were a child? Or have you mellowed and matured, come into some of your own authority, so that you can relate to your parents more as equals now?

It is probably more difficult to spot the occasions when you catch yourself behaving as these people used to. These familiar figures may be showing how you have taken on board their way of being, whether you like it or not, and that you are unconsciously acting it out, in dreams and in waking. One of the prime functions of our dreams is to wake us up to ourselves.

A sure way of recognizing a sub-personality is when someone else's behaviour triggers a particularly strong emotional response in us. It may be that they are behaving in ways we don't allow ourselves, or refuse to admit to. Here is a chance to learn just how we have limited our life by rejecting certain kinds of experience. We may also recognize our reactive judgmental attitudes too, when we hear ourselves exclaim, 'How dare he?', 'Who does she think she is?', 'How disgusting!', and so on.

When there is a more positive projection onto someone, we might say, 'He's so reliable and strong', 'She's so kind', 'She never has a bad word to say about anyone', 'He's very clever', or 'He's amazingly supportive'. We may see these people as many things: gifted, lucky, intelligent, and creative (we're especially good at giving away our own creativity!), but if all we can do is praise them, what we are doing is putting them up on a pedestal, a precarious and sometimes lonely place to be.

Often what these people or dream characters are doing is living the life we would like to live, but continually deny. What they take for granted may seem risky and therefore threatening to our ego. We then either resent or admire them for it, but in truth we can grow only when we start to take on these qualities for ourselves.

In dreams, a genuine sub-personality will certainly appear more than once. They may not always be exactly the same, but several different characters in a series of dreams will be of a similar type. Noting what they have in common will help you to see that a sub-personality is emerging into consciousness. Eventually you will meet this aspect of yourself as a clear, identifiable sub-personality as these characters coalesce.

Some sub-personalities are instantly recognizable, perhaps because they carry a strong, clear type of energy or role, or maybe because they evoke a strong response in us. Others will remind you of how you sometimes are in waking, perhaps when you are caught off guard.

Dream characters who appear as sub-personalities are often a little exaggerated, perhaps larger than life. Because each one represents only one aspect of the personality, it is possible to identify them clearly. Here lies our passion, our ability to laugh freely, dance, sing, paint, play the drums, have good sex, and speak our truth.

A schoolteacher, for instance, may have developed a strong teacher sub-personality who behaves in dreams just as he or she does at work. Some other aspects may not have been given so much energy and attention, though. This part of us will then feature in our dreams, seeking our recognition and cooperation. I am reminded of one teacher who had an uninhibited stripper sub-personality in her dreams. She cheerfully admitted that it was something she'd always had a secret desire to do! A doctor who needed focus and gravity in his work had a very lively, fun loving, and slightly irresponsible practical joker sub-personality who would come out to play, in dreams and sometimes in waking too.

We all have a darker, shadow side to our make-up as well, as I have already mentioned. What we hide here includes our anger, cruelty, guilt, fear, jealousy, and brutality. Most of us are aware of characteristics that we are ashamed of, if we are honest. Each one of us has the potential for the very best and the very worst of human nature. The ego may say 'no' to this darker side being acted out, but a healthy ego will not deny the shadow's existence.

In making such shadow sub-personalities conscious we must not feel that we have to get rid of them, or necessarily transform them, either. We need to accept them as part of our personality and find ways to relate to them. This may involve finding some more constructive role for them, or building an appropriate inner container in which to hold them. Their value is in being who they are, part of our wholeness. In working with sub-personalities we are aiming for:

• self-discovery;
• ease in relationships;
• enhanced self-awareness;
• resolving inner conflict;
• realizing more of our potential;
• the testing and reorganizing of our boundaries;
• informing the ego in its choice-making process.

We can do this by relating well to the sub-personalities we find, and then by helping them to relate to each other. When we encounter a difficult sub-personality and realize the powerful though subtle effect it has had on our life's journey, we can be left feeling helpless and ineffectual. The patterns can feel so strongly established that we may wonder how we can possibly do anything about it.

But you only need be open to change, and to have plenty of persistence! You need to see that you can't do it all from the ego position alone. Often the ego has been conditioned by a troublesome sub-personality for much of your life, which will naturally limit your ways of responding. A fresh perspective is needed. Usually, if we have a sub-personality which behaves in one particular way, there will be another, opposite, sub-personality who can come in and counter its effect, supporting the ego. Here is some recent work from my own inner process, which may help to illustrate this point.

Going deeper into your process

In Transformative Dreamwork we begin with the original dream then open ourselves up to its insights and messages using whatever skills and techniques suggest themselves. Many people who are new to dreamwork will write out their dream, try one technique, learn a little, then think that they've finished with that dream, and move on to the next. This is fine, since the next dream they have will offer a different view of the same theme anyway. But with more experience you will learn to travel further with each individual dream, letting it stay close to consciousness, moving through several phases of work with it, and going deeper into your process.

We don't have to make anything happen, but simply remain alert and sensitive to the current theme as it presents itself in our waking lives, recognizing opportunities to return to the dream message. The following dream I had helps to explain this.

'I'm with a smiling African woman, in a clearing at the centre of a compound of village huts. There is a big old blackened cooking pot in front of us on the warm red earth. She's probably about forty, dressed in simple but brightly coloured robes, with a scarf twisted into a turban on her head. She laughs a lot and doesn't seem to have a care in the world.

"C'mon girl, hunker down here with me, we got things to do!" she says. I squat on my haunches next to her in the dust. I like her easy manner, vitality, and her sense of fun. She's like a breath of fresh air. Other women walk over to join us. It seems that we will sit talking of women's things in a circle, and maybe we'll eat together.'

The process: part one

This lovely earthy woman came to me in this dream at a time when my focus was on doing some bodywork to try to relieve persistent tension in my neck and shoulders. I was seeing Lucy Lidell, a local therapist and dreamworker who has created a wonderful way of working with the body, combining massage with following the imagery which can be evoked in response to healing touch.

After my African woman dream, in a session where Lucy was working on my tight shoulders and neck, I got an image of a grey suited, cold, stern man standing right behind me. He had my neck firmly gripped in his big hand, almost lifting me off my feet so that only my toes touched the floor. Though I'd never met this character before I knew instantly that he'd been holding me like this for a very long time, without my ever realizing. I recognized from childhood experience the frozen fearful state caused by being immobilized like this. I felt the old tightening in my stomach and upper body.

Under his suit, this man seemed to be made of tin, a little like the Tin Man from *The Wizard of Oz*, who didn't have a heart! His body felt completely rigid and set in his way of being, and mine was now affected in the same way. I realized that he reminded me of my mother!

Governed by a similar inner masculine figure herself, she had a very erect, self-conscious posture that I had naturally emulated as a child and young woman. It spoke of her inhibitions and her need to get everything right, which inevitably led to her becoming a controlling personality. Sadly, she spent all of her life held fast in this grip, as I have endured it in mine.

Hating being held in this helpless position, I was trying to reason with the uncommunicative man when suddenly, there was the African woman from my dream, spluttering with laughter! She almost danced around him, saying, 'Well, would you look at this! He's from another time and place, this one! Just look at the state of him!' poking him playfully with her forefinger and chuckling gleefully all the time. Her good humoured curiosity was infectious, and I started to 'lighten up', too. The woman's disparaging remarks and refusal to be intimidated by him cut him 'down to size'. He appeared confused and less sure of himself.

I would never have thought of inviting her in to help me. I was actually trying to persuade him to release his grip on me in a very reasonable, psychology textbook-correct manner. In his way, in other words! So in still working to 'get it right', I was still wrong! But the woman's earthy irreverence cut through the deadly stalemate and woke me up to myself.

Whenever this inner man grabbed me by the neck I unconsciously regressed into the fearful child I used to be, hemmed in by do's and don'ts, trying hard to get things right to avoid my mother's disapproval and possible punishment. He held me as if I were a rabbit or kitten, so that they become transfixed and cannot move.

My new African friend showed me that if I could regard him from my confident, less formal, adult feminine self, I could release the hold he had over me. I followed through by telling him I would no longer be held in that way. I let him know he was harming my body and that I had no need of his protection from wrongdoing. No one can ever again frighten my child in the old way. That danger has passed. I get lots of things wrong now and that's okay. I'm human, that's all! As I write, I feel the African woman's chuckle rising within me.

As the visualization (and the massage therapy session), came to an end, the woman gave me a pot. It was a big fired clay bowl, a practical thing, not meant for use in ritual or ceremony. 'It's for making things in,' she said. 'You could start with bread.'

I ended the visualization pleased to have met her again, deeply valuing her and happy with my gift. I like making bread, though I don't often find time for it. I bought flour and yeast, but other things needed my attention, so I postponed the bread making.

The process: part two
A few days later, in the bath, where I often reflect on my dreamwork, I became aware of the tin man again. My neck and shoulders had been tight all day and I felt his unyielding presence strongly in my body. I spoke to him, adult to adult, from the depths of my soul, weary of the way he could still affect my body even though I had now identified him and understood what was happening.

I told him I was no longer the child he thought me to be. I reminded him that I did not now need his protection and that I wanted him to let go. Knowing how much of his way I had inherited from my mother, I commanded him to return to her, from whence he came. When we can make such a choice from a loving heart we can begin to change an inherited ancestral emotional and psychic pattern. When we do this, as many people are now choosing to do, we begin to heal not only ourselves, but the ancestors.

A part of this healing is acknowledging the part you have played in perpetuating this behaviour for yourself. So I returned to the tin man now, knowing for certain that a part of him, the part I had unknowingly cultivated for myself, belonged with me and was indeed mine.

Having sent away my mother's unwanted gift to me, I felt some of the tension leaving my body and a sense of more space opening up around me. But my own tin man still held me fast in that robotic grip. I told him he must let me go, imagining prising loose first one finger then another. He stood, uncertain now, flexing his stiffened right hand and arm. I felt a moment's compassion – he'd been caught in the same grim dynamic too, all these years!

I reassured him that I could find a place and a new role for him in my life, and that I could value his strength of will, his persistence, and devotion to his task. He looked again at his clawed hand. 'What else can I possibly do with this?' I knew that he needed something practical to do to ease the stiffness in his hand, before anything else. Then I understood. I chuckled. 'You and I are going to make some bread', I said, and I marvelled at the innate intelligence which knows long before the ego does exactly what is needed.

The process: part three

It's interesting that the African woman – the antidote – appeared with just what was needed before the image of the tin man. I see the woman as a sub-personality too now. I can recognize both as valid, reflecting as they do two very different ways of being. There is a fun-loving woman inside of me who appears from time to time. Yet the African woman brings in something foreign from a different continent, to enrich my experience of this part of myself. Many westerners are dreaming now of such people: Africans, North American Indians, Malaysians, and people from India. They each carry different qualities, according to their individual culture, that can bring in a refreshing perception of whatever inner process we are working through.

When you have such figures in your dreams and begin to feel they may suggest a sub-personality, you could try writing out a list of key words to describe them. So my African woman might be spontaneous, flowing, fun loving, free and easy, irreverent, down-to-earth, instinctual, colourful, and secure in her self-knowledge.

The tin man, by contrast, could be seen as stiff-necked, defensive, heartless, proper, rigid, determined, closed, grey, and so stuck within his limited vision that he had very little discernible sense of self. I know that at times I can be some or all of these things, but I'd like more of her and less of him in my life now.

Intellectually I had understood long ago the limiting and inhibiting effect my mother's way of being had upon me. I have worked at freeing myself from her grip, learning to think for myself, to enjoy the flow of my feelings, to let go of my fear, so becoming less formal and defended. But the body takes longer. Its pace is slower. Its cells hold the imprint of everything we have experienced, and the body neither lies nor forgets.

I have always taken my body for granted and it has been a good body. Now that I'm getting older, it is making me more aware of its vulnerability. Because I am intuitive, my body was always going to be the last to get my attention. That's just the way of it. Now that I have made the acquaintance of these two sub-personalities and I have an image for what has been happening to my body as a result of being unconsciously caught, I really feel that things can begin to change. It won't happen overnight – the body will still take its time! But soon enough I know I'll feel the physical benefits of this new piece of work.

Using visualization in dreamwork

Many of the techniques involved in dreamwork require you to go back into your dreams using visualization skills. Quite often people who are inexperienced at revisiting the dream or using visualization in this way will question the results, asking, 'Am I making all of this up, do you think?'

I usually answer, 'Well, perhaps you are. We know so little about the vagaries of the imagination. But of all the things you might have come up with, I wonder why you chose to imagine that particular thing, which began as puzzling but became so meaningful?'

A good way of affirming that your experience is authentic is when you find yourself genuinely surprised by the people and events in your imagery. I was surprised by the arrival of the African woman and confused by the form taken by the tin man, even though I immediately knew his affect was familiar. My conscious imagination might have conjured up something much more predictable.

Another way of knowing that what you find is true is that it rings true in the moment, during the visualization, and holds up to scrutiny later as you review your experience. In the early stages this is something else you may have to take on trust for a while. Give yourself and your Dream Maker time to let things become clear. With sub-personalities, as with other dream characters or the people you newly meet in waking, the old maxim applies. By their fruits ye shall know them!

I'd like to move on now to lead you into your own experience of this phase of dreamwork by doing a couple of exercises in meeting a dream character. This will involve revisiting your dream, the use of visualization, or creative imagination (also known as active imagination), and moving into an altered state of consciousness. It's counterproductive to try to read instructions as you go, since this tends to move you into your head, which then takes over so that you lose the imaginative flow. This applies too to making notes of your experience. It is better by far to read the exercise through to get to know it, then return to the dream and let the experience of meeting your dream character unfold. Only make notes afterward. Don't worry about not being able to hold enough of what happens. On some level you will retain it, even if not all of it is immediately brought into conscious awareness.

Exercise nine: meeting a dream character
Part one
• Choose a dream that has a character you'd like to know more about, but not a frightening one for a first attempt.

• Do all your groundwork with the dream before beginning this exercise. Make associations and connections with what happens in the dream and the character you have chosen. You will feel more confident if you know what there is to know about this person from your dream before you go in to meet them, just as you would want some background information before meeting someone new in waking.

• Begin now to get some clear sense of why you want to return to the dream and what questions you want to ask this dream figure.

• Before moving on to the next part of the exercise, remember to work in an environment where you won't be disturbed. When you move into an altered state of consciousness by returning to the dream, any interruption can be quite shocking and disorientating. Give yourself a mental time limit. Fifteen minutes is quite enough, plus time to make notes as the exercise ends.

Part two

• Sitting quietly for a moment, get in touch with your breathing, allowing its steady rhythm to lead you into a quiet, calm, inner space.

• Review the dream in your mind's eye, with the character you have chosen as your focus. You are about to re-enter the dream. Remember to go in open and alert, willing to listen to the other's point of view, suspending disbelief and letting yourself surrender to the experience.

• Choose a point in the dream where you are with this person and can see them clearly. Let yourself become the 'you' in the dream, or simply imagine yourself moving into the dream, if you were not originally there. Greet the dream character. Just saying 'hello' will do to let them know that you are there.

• Note how you are feeling in relation to the other person. Are you upset, angry, puzzled, or happy to see them? You might share these feelings with them, giving time for them to respond. Or you might ask what it is that brings this person into your dream now. Again, wait for a response, just as you would in a waking meeting.

• Though you may have some important questions, you can also learn a lot by just listening to the response you are getting, and taking your cue from that. This is a more sensitive and relational way to be, rather than ploughing on with a preconceived agenda, regardless of the reply. Eventually a natural flow will develop in your conversation, as it might do in waking.

• Sometimes words just aren't adequate, and a sympathetic touch of the hand or a hug will speak volumes. Joining in whatever activity the character is engaged can be a good way to get to know them. On a few occasions I have wordlessly danced with a dream character, mirroring their movements, and beginning to feel how that person feels.

• Whether you are simply talking together, sharing a task, or mirroring what your character is doing, find a moment to ask this person if there is something they want of you, something they'd like you to do. Think about what might be involved before you agree to it. If what is being asked feels too much or too difficult, say so, and ask if there is something easier that you could do first. For whatever you agree to do in such inner meetings will need to be carried out, perhaps in waking, as a mark of mutual respect and trust within this new relationship. You will be answering a request here, not blindly carrying out some directive. If you have a powerful character who seems to want to tell you what to do, you have the right to refuse, and to call in a dream helper to support you, or to terminate the meeting. Your dream characters are usually cooperative, if a little enigmatic, when you meet them in this way.

• Now ask what gift this person brings into your dream and your life. This may be a symbolic offering. Try not to reject anything as unsuitable. Stay open and accepting, for the meaning of the gift may become clear on reflection.

• This may be a good point to leave this first meeting. Take the opportunity to thank the dream figure for being with you on this occasion, even if the meeting was a difficult one, and say goodbye in whatever way feels right for you both. You may want to agree to meet again, to get to know each other better. You can choose to do this in further exercises.

• Leave the dream, once again becoming fully aware of your breathing. Open your eyes and look around at the room, coming back into yourself and your surroundings. Have a stretch, or get up and move about for a moment or two, getting in touch with your body but keeping the spirit of what you have just experienced.

• When you are ready, write up the experience in your dream journal.

Reflections on exercise nine

These meetings with dream characters can be full of meaning and insight, which sometimes comes as we make our notes, as well as during the experience. If this technique didn't work for you, try again with another dream figure. It may well be that the strangeness of this way of working puts you off. Or perhaps you don't visualize easily. I find this difficulty is more common in men than women, in the groups that I run. Here is another approach, which may work better for you.

Exercise ten: working with cushions

• Having chosen your character and done your groundwork, select a cushion to represent the dream figure, and another one for yourself. (You may prefer to do this using two chairs.) Place them at a distance that feels comfortable to you, then sit on 'your' cushion, looking at the other, knowing it is the place of your dream character. You may even find yourself actually seeing the person sitting on the cushion.

• Begin as in the previous exercise, greeting the character and telling them how you feel about their presence in your dream. You might want to ask your first question too. Then move over to sit on the other cushion, knowing that as you do, you will become this dream person, having heard what has just been said to you. Now let yourself respond from this person's place, letting them speak through you.

• When a natural pause comes into the conversation, move back to your own cushion and receive what the character has had to say, then respond. Keep moving between the two, letting the conversation find its natural flow.

• Always be sure to end the exercise on your own cushion, as yourself. We don't want you unconsciously leaving this piece of work wearing the dream character's persona! When you are sure you are back fully as yourself, and in touch with your body and surroundings, begin to make your notes.

Reflections on exercise ten

Take time to consider what has happened between you and the dream character. This will be but a small part of an ongoing process, and there will certainly be some follow-up to your taking this step towards your unconscious in the next few dreams. There may be some synchronicity in outer life too, as something is reflected back to you in waking coincidences. Stay alert to these affirmations of your work, and add them to your journal notes.

What theme is becoming clear to you now? How does what you have learned from this exercise help you to connect with your current dream theme and inner processes? Has your understanding of the character changed as a result of this meeting? Do you feel that you know them better now?

Don't say too much to others about this inner process, or what you have found in the exercise until you have had time to digest it and know it for yourself. People who aren't involved in this type of work may not understand, and their remarks can be hurtful to the vulnerable part of you that is eager to learn and grow.

If you agreed to do something for your dream character, be sure to do it, preferably within the next few days. Never agree to do anything that contradicts your own moral or ethical standards or is unlawful.

How has this exercise left you feeling about yourself? Do you like the way you were in the dream and this meeting? Or are you feeling a little crestfallen or ashamed, perhaps because your ego has taken a bit of a knock? Remember not to be too hard on yourself or the other character, nor too full of praise if things have gone well. Take it easy, wait, and see what the next dream will bring.

five 5 *Finding your symbols*

A symbol is a thing of mystery. Beyond its obvious everyday meaning, any symbol speaks of something deep and obscure. This sense of a hidden meaning exerts a fascination that may attract or repel, but is difficult to ignore. As we contemplate a symbol, something deep within us stirs in response.

Vital to human beings since our beginnings, symbols are a direct communication from the unconscious, in its language, bringing knowledge that the conscious mind alone cannot fully comprehend. We could not possibly understand the full implications of everything that happens to us day after day. Yet nothing is lost, for the unconscious mind stores all of our experiences. Alerted by something significant that has eluded our consciousness, this inner intelligence springs into action. Memories of our personal past experience are drawn to the current one. This in turn acts as a magnet, attracting associated information from our collective history. The whole then takes shape as an individual symbol, designed to catch our attention and strike a chord within.

It is easy to see how symbols have gathered a generally accepted universal meaning through the ages, linking us as they do with the wisdom of the collective unconscious. This helps us to understand the wider significance of concepts that we might otherwise fail to grasp. However, it is not enough to settle for the universal meaning as an explanation of the message your symbol brings, for any symbol that comes to you will also carry layers of profound personal meaning, meant for you alone.

A symbol is expansive and multi-faceted, requiring time for reflection if it is to yield up its fullness to our quest for meaning. We have to abandon the ego's tendency to identify, label, and move on. We must give up even the search for meaning at times, allowing ourselves instead to savour the experience of just being with the symbol. This highly intimate personal connection with any symbol brings depth and spaciousness to the inner journey.

Symbols and signs

Once we understand the energetic vitality of symbols we are less likely to confuse them with signs. A sign may be instantly recognizable, conveying meaning through the familiarity of common usage. The emblem on a badge will be a sign of the wearer's involvement with a particular organization, but is not a symbol. Trademarks declare sole ownership of a product, safeguarding the manufacturer's rights. Names of organisations may be abbreviated to initials, for example NATO and FBI. While these are universally recognizable, they are basically just a quicker way to establish identity. Road signs alert us to the conditions ahead, using simple images. That is all they do. Nothing more is implied.

Symbols have inspired the themes of artists, writers, choreographers, composers, and architects the world over. Analytical and transpersonal psychology, along with other branches of the healing arts, draw upon symbol as a creative source of guidance which can illuminate the psyche, supporting their understanding of their clients' journeys. These same symbols can also be used manipulatively, as advertisers and politicians are only too aware.

Drawing upon an established universal symbol, the British Labour Party chose the red rose for its updated logo to project its image of New Labour. With its connotations of unity, perfection, and passion, and rather more genteel association with English gardens, the rose gives a softer, warmer impression than the old red flag of Labour, and is designed to win new, more middle-class people over to this traditionally working-class party.

The Jolly Green Giant on tins of a certain brand of sweetcorn is a distortion of the Green Man mentioned in chapter one. In this programme the hero, when angered, gained superhuman strength and musculature, and turned green as he split his shirt! Of course sweetcorn and television are not universal symbols in themselves, but they evoke our subliminal awareness of the vitality of a powerful symbolic figure as an inducement to buy, or to tune in.

Almost all religions use symbolism to communicate and intensify religious experience. Indeed, such great religious books as the Bible, Koran, and Talmud may be seen as profound symbolic works. Places of worship symbolically reach up towards heaven with soaring arches, domes, minarets, and spires. We find 'mother church' filled with icons, candles, and flowers. Circles feature in sacred places, perhaps as a rose window, or mandala, expressing the concept of wholeness and the totality of the Self.

In Christianity, the primary symbol is the cross, reminding us of the suffering and death of Jesus followed by the miracle of the resurrection. In some cultures the sun carries this symbolic religious function. Its life-giving power has been recognized and worshipped from the time of our earliest ancestors, who watched it 'die' each night, only to be reborn with the dawning of each new day.

The total eclipse in parts of Europe in August 1999 would have terrified our primitive forbears, threatening the end of all life on earth. The power of the sun symbol has carried through from the Egyptian pharaohs, the sun gods of South American Indians and other tribal peoples to modern day Japan, where the Shinto religion deifies the sun.

Jung explains, 'Because there are innumerable things beyond the range of human understanding, we constantly use symbolic terms to represent concepts that we cannot define or fully comprehend. This is one reason why all religions employ symbolic language or images. But this conscious use of symbols is only one aspect of a psychological fact of great importance: man also produces symbols unconsciously and spontaneously, in the form of dreams' (from *Man and his Symbols*).

One of the great universal symbols to emerge from the long tradition of remembering and working with dreams is the spider, Iktome, the keeper of dreams, also known as the dream weaver in some North American Indian traditions. Iktome weaves her web to catch our dreams for us. Some say she catches and saves the good ones, filtering out the bad ones as we sleep. Others believe that she catches all the night's dreams, good or bad, keeping them for the dreamer to remember on waking. Some Native Americans make dream catchers, in the shape of a spider's web, to hang in their sleeping area. They place a special feather or bead at the centre of the web to represent Iktome, watching and waiting for the dreams to come.

You can make your own dream catcher, hanging feathers or small objects from it to symbolize special dreams that you have worked with, or you could buy one, as many are now commercially available. But be very careful what you bring into your sleeping area – if you are buying a dream catcher, take a little time to sense its energy. If it doesn't feel good, don't buy it. When you find the right one, place it thoughtfully in your bedroom, knowing that it is a symbol to help you remember your dreams.

What is it that makes the common spider so symbolic? Many people are afraid of spiders, perhaps sensing something of the dark aspect of the Great Mother as a weaver of destiny. She carries the attributes of mythological figures such as the Greek moon goddess Athena, weaver of the world, and of the three Fates, the Moirai, who spin, measure, and cut the thread of destiny. In Hindu and Buddhist traditions she is Maya, weaver of the web of illusion, and may represent the universal Creator, weaving the world from the thread of its own substance.

The spider's web was likened to the wheel of fate, with the spider a goddess at the hub of her wheel. We admire the spider's ability to weave her web, a delicate thing of beauty. But there is a stickiness to it, too. Perhaps the web of Iktome holds the dreams long enough for us to remain with them, and free ourselves from the illusions of the waking ego. In the dream catcher mode she is not seen as the Devourer, but as a helper at the transition between sleep and waking.

If you are really phobic about spiders and cannot relate to Iktome at all, you may like to consider the owl as a dream symbol. Sacred to Athena, the owl represents wisdom, and some tribal peoples see it as the bringer of dreams. But this symbol also has its dark face, being associated in many mythologies with death and desolation. Because dreams come in the night, brought out of the darkness of the unconscious, from the unknown, they have become linked with nocturnal creatures that know the ways of the night and the dark.

Symbols are one of the great gifts of the dream, bringing rich new layers of depth and meaning, and new challenges too! For as we go to meet the dream to learn more about our symbols, we take a step closer to the unconscious. We have to literally 'get out of our minds' to relate to a symbol. We cannot rely upon reason and logic, but must let the symbol seduce us into communicating with the dream in its own way, the way of the unconscious.

A new way to see symbols

The symbolic language of dreams is very subtle, carrying much more than is immediately apparent to us as we awaken. We need to be equally subtle in our approach, resisting the more fixed path of intellectual interpretation, which can be reductive and relatively shallow. If you have a dream dictionary, throw it away, or at least lose it for the time being! Having someone else tell you what your dream symbol means will close you down, tempting you to accept this as the only authentic explanation and then causing you to tailor your dream to fit this apparent meaning.

It is better to stay open and enquiring around your symbol. Approach it from all angles, looking, learning, and questioning. Move and flow with its energies, sifting through layers until you arrive, by degrees and all manner of means, at your own unique place of knowing. In this way you become less passive, enjoying the delight of discovering your own insights. Here are a few examples from former students of mine:

The lone wolf

'*A wolf is roaming the streets and I watch him, holding out my hand.*'

From *Little Red Riding Hood* to the book *Women Who Run With The Wolves*, the possible interpretations of wolf as symbol are great and varied. But by staying with the dream, we learn that this is a lone wolf, a sorry state for a pack animal. It is also distanced from its natural environment or home. Working with this, the dreamer immediately saw its relevance to her feelings of estrangement from her family, who live in another land, close to a forest. She has become the outcast and at times feels a keen sense of rejection and loneliness.

Animals also represent our instinctual wild nature. The dreamer went on to work at this deeper level, examining her lack of trust and estrangement from such an important part of herself. The hopeful sign is that she is holding out her hand, unafraid of the wolf instinct.

The clam shell

'I am walking along the seashore, with a small girl of about two years old beside me. I find a clam, tightly closed. I wonder if there will be a pearl inside it, but I don't know how to get it open. The little girl shows me how, using another shell to prise the clam open. Inside is not just one pearl but lots, about a dozen. I am astonished.'

The clam is closed, suggesting that the dreamer is clammed up. The shell is hard and protective of the soft interior. The dreamer was interested in the treasure that the clam, once opened, may yield. In working with the dream, the pearls became '...pearls of wisdom, from deep within'.

It was the tiny child who knew how to open the shell. Here is a child who can access her inner wisdom, leading the way for the adult who may have built such a hard shell around herself that she has lost touch with her own inner wisdom.

The lamb

'I am in a ploughed garden (with furrows in the flowerbeds) near a house. There are winding paths around these flowerbeds. As I walk along one of them I see a lamb frozen in a furrow – or so it seems.'

The lamb is the Christian symbol of the most vulnerable of the flock and a universal symbol for the child. There is an incongruence in finding it 'frozen in a furrow' and separated not only from the flock, but also from its mother. The dreamer recognized this within the dream, which continues: 'He is clearly weak and tiny. I take him in and feed him and warm him. Later, I see his mother with many other lambs and return him to his family.'

So the dreamer acts as an archetypal Good Shepherd or Samaritan, nurturing and protecting the lamb. The personal and universal meanings are the same. In rescuing the lamb without being possessive, the dreamer fulfils the function of the Self.

Identifying your dream symbols

You may now be starting to identify and think about your own dream symbols. Some symbols appear strikingly, and are easily identifiable as such. Others may emerge slowly, gathering energy as they go. If this is the case, you may have several dreams with similar objects, situations, or relationships in them. Gradually, from dream to dream, a theme or motif of a symbolic nature will become clear. Alternatively, you might meet the same type of people, dream after dream. Eventually, these dream characters may coalesce into one symbolic figure or group of people who carry some symbolic connotation.

Composite figures, as we saw chapter four, are common in dreams, appearing as someone known to the dreamer, yet different. This maybe partly an outer and partly a dream figure, or a combination of two people we know, indicating that we are not meant to take the figure too literally as simply representing the person we know. It is better to consider the attributes, qualities, or behaviour of both characters, and see where that leads you.

Symptoms as symbols

Since most of us have little physical presence in our dream life, when symptoms come to draw our attention to some part of the body, they are seldom literal, but are more often metaphorical. Such dreams show us how the emotions that we cannot or do not allow ourselves to express come to rest in the body, building up over a period of time, eventually causing discomfort or illness. If you habitually store stress in your neck and shoulders, when the pressure becomes too much, you may dream of wearing a yoke. A person over-burdened by responsibilities may be struggling uphill carrying a loaded backpack or heavy luggage. An aching head may be gripped in a vice. Feelings of anxiety or dread may be experienced as the weight of a heavy stone in the belly. These are often manifested in the body on waking, but we may just take painkillers and get on with the day. If this happens to you, try talking to your symptom, asking it what it represents, and what it needs. Then try to meet this need. Just sitting and breathing gently into the painful or uncomfortable area can be a great help.

When something is seriously wrong physically, the Dream Maker may ease the impact of this knowledge by showing an animal suffering in a similar way (see Emma's dream on page 19). In finding compassion for the dream animal, you will unconsciously relate to, and help, the suffering part of yourself. Animals, which are creatures of instinct and at home in their bodies, often appear symbolizing this aspect of ourselves in our dreams. They can be symbols of recovery from illness, too.

The following is an example of such a dream. Jane, a dedicated nurse, had taken time off work through total exhaustion. When she had rested for a few weeks and was beginning to wonder if she was well enough to go back to work, she had this dream:

'I am in my bedroom, sitting up in bed and watching two tiny creatures playing on the floor. They are squirrel-like, but not squirrels and they are full of playful energy. My dogs come in and start chasing around the room with them – it's great fun.'

On waking, Jane was pleased with this dream, knowing it affirmed the return of her own vitality. It was indeed time to return to work.

If your dreams are making you aware of physical symptoms, please always seek medical help. It would be disrespectful to your body to recognize the emotional or psychological meaning of a symptom at the expense of the physical, and could lead to something more serious.

Whether your symbols come as objects, people, relationships, situations, or symptoms, you will know your them by their affect. Symbols have a kind of emotional charge. You may feel intrigued, wanting to know more, sensing that there is much more to discover about something or someone in your dream. Sometimes we recognize a symbol as we recall a dream, but often it is not until we write the dream into our journal and begin to work with it that the symbolic content becomes apparent.

If something appears out of place in the dream setting, it may catch our attention, as in Ruth's dream which took place in a swimming pool. She wrote:

'While swimming, I noticed a dark shape lying at the bottom of the pool. I thought it was a tile, to begin with. Writing the dream in my journal, I began to feel that the 'tile' might be a sort of shield. I didn't know why it held so much energy for me, but I was curious and decided to go back into the dream to have a closer look at it.

'I swam down to the bottom and picked up the 'tile'. As I did so, it was as if it had been acting as a plug and the water emptied out of the pool! I saw I was holding not a tile or shield, but a chain-mail gauntlet, the palm of which was slightly torn. This surprised and puzzled me and I came out of the dream again to make notes of what I'd found.

'I considered whether this meant that someone had 'thrown down the gauntlet' in some kind of challenge to me, but this didn't feel right. It was when I reread these notes that I misread something. I'd written that the gauntlet had a tear in the palm. This time I read it as a tear (as in weeping), which felt right. It somehow made sense, and everything fell into place as I realized the vulnerability of the owner of the glove. I felt it might be showing me another side of my own inner masculine defender, and I wanted to meet this aspect of him, to get to know him more. So, I went back into the dream, inviting him to meet me there.

'This time I found myself alone in a vast expanse of barren ground, feeling a bit frightened. A strange noise unnerved me and I saw a rock some distance away begin to move, changing shape to become a formidable Samurai warrior. Seeing that I was afraid, the warrior used his sword to make a circle in the earth around him.

'We seemed to communicate telepathically, and I understood that this boundary was to protect me from being overwhelmed by his powerful energy. But I gradually realized it was also to protect him, as he began to take off all his armour and clothes, making himself very vulnerable. I knew he was teaching me something valuable by doing this – that true strength and power only comes when we can acknowledge our vulnerability. This felt as if it was the whole point of our meeting in this way. Thanking him for all that he did for me, I left the dream.'

This skilled piece of dreamwork is a wonderful illustration of the combination of openness and persistence required at this level. Ruth was intrigued by something in her dream, but didn't realize she had a symbol until she found the gauntlet, which further puzzled her by its incongruence within the dream setting. It was only from reading what she had written of her first dream re-entry that the unexpected meaning of the symbol began to emerge. Here the dual meaning of the word 'tear' led her to understand that the message was connected to the inseparability of strength and vulnerability. All through this work, Ruth trusted her own sense of the symbol's meaning, and the integrity of her dream.

The symbol moved through several changes. Ruth didn't initiate these changes or try to control the dream in any way. Perhaps she had already intuited something of what was to come when she perceived the 'tile' as a possible shield, another attribute of the warrior figure. When she removed the gauntlet from the bottom of the pool, something watery, perhaps emotional, was unblocked. She had metaphorically 'pulled the plug'.

Next she found the dual message of the gauntlet, the original true symbol, but carrying the 'tear' to lead her to the recognition of vulnerability where she might least expect it. This, of course, was a current theme for Ruth at the time of the dream. Many of us find it difficult to move from extreme vulnerability into our true strength and power, because we feel that these qualities are polarized. The waking ego might see it so, but the wisdom of the unconscious mind knows otherwise, as is demonstrated in the Samurai's message.

Even the sub-personality of the Samurai warrior, which the symbol led to, changed from its original form of a rock. This is another metaphor, as he helped Ruth to understand that he is her rock, and that she could rely on him totally, before he risked allowing her to see him naked. She felt that this was without threat or any sexual implication, emphasized by his creating the 'sacred space' in the earth around himself.

How helpful it is to know that we have an amazing power to create a sacred, protective circle around ourselves when we have to go into situations that can make us vulnerable! Not only that, but somewhere within all of us we may find the compassion to contain our own energy and power in a similar way when we see that it frightens other people.

Ruth flowed between conscious and unconscious in her dreamwork, returning to the dream using exercise nine 'meeting a dream character' (see page 83). She communicated telepathically with the Samurai in order to help her find out more about her symbols. Following is another exercise that may help you to gain confidence when choosing to go back into a dream to meet a symbol.

Exercise eleven: meeting your symbol

You will need your dream journal and pen and, at least forty five minutes of completely uninterrupted time. If you are alone in the house, turn down the phone, and decide not to answer the door.

If, during this exercise, you feel afraid, remember that you can make choices. Do you remember how Ruth's Samurai warrior created a sacred circle around himself? You can do that too. Just visualize a circle of bright white light all around you, keeping you safe. Nothing and no one can cross into your circle without your permission. Knowing this may help you to stay with the image of the symbol. If you still don't feel safe, you can choose to abandon this exercise, and just sit quietly, pondering upon what frightens you so.

• Choose a dream that contains a symbol you'd like to explore, but not a frightening one. You don't have to take unnecessary risks in dreamwork. Let a safer symbol start you off.

• Reading your dream through, take time to make associations and connections. In this way, you gain some understanding of the dream as the context for your symbol. **This is essential preparation before any of the techniques that take you into altered states of consciousness.**

• Spend no more than ten minutes on this next part, followed by some time for journal work. A time boundary is important at this fascinating stage, because you may be seduced into staying too long in the visualization that follows.

• With this in mind, choose a moment in the dream where you can see the symbol clearly, and stop the action of the dream at that point, rather like using the pause button on a video recorder.

• Let your awareness move into the dream, and begin to experience yourself in relation to your symbol. Does the distance between you and your symbol feel comfortable? If not, move back or forward a little, so that you can see the symbol clearly without being overwhelmed by its energy. Are you experiencing any strong feelings, emotions, or reactions, now that you've reached this point?

• When you are ready to continue with the exercise, just stay where you are and take a good look at this symbol. Does it look the same now as it did when you remembered the dream? Has anything changed? In your imagination, take a walk all around the symbol. In the dream you may only have seen it from one angle. Now you can see all of it. How does it seem now?

• Move closer, or touch your symbol if it feels appropriate. How does its texture feel to you as you touch it? Is it warm or cold, rough or smooth, fixed or pliable? Does it have a smell, or sound? If appropriate, would you like to taste it? How are you feeling now in this close proximity to your symbol? Has any emotion intensified or changed in any way? Perhaps you're not feeling anything.

• Step back a little way and look at the symbol afresh. What have you learned about it? How does that affect your relationship with it? Speak to your symbol of all of this. Let it know how you first perceived it, what you have recognized in this meeting with it, and how you feel about it now. Give time for the symbol to respond. Listen to what the symbol has to say. Ask it what gift it brings you through appearing in this manner. Thank the symbol for this gift, and ask is there anything it needs from you. If it asks for too much, tell the symbol this, and ask for something simpler. (As a mark of your integrity within your inner work, if you agree to do something a symbol asks you, you should follow through by doing it as soon as you can.)

• For the final stage in this exercise, imagine that you move closer to your symbol, so close that you can just meld, moving into the symbol for a moment or two. What impression do you get of how it is to be this symbol, in this dream? Try to see the dream, and the dreamer through the eyes of the symbol. Locate a sense of the energy and quality of the symbol itself.

• When you are ready, come back into yourself in the dream, and take a last look at the symbol. Thank the symbol for being there with you, and let it know how you value it now. Allow yourself to see the dream move through to its conclusion, just as it did when you first remembered it. Perhaps something in the dream will have changed as a result of the interaction you've just experienced, perhaps not.

• Bring yourself fully back into an awareness of your body and the room, while keeping a sense of the energy of your symbol. What have you learned through this process of relating to your symbol? How can you use this knowledge in waking life? Write in your journal as much as you can of what you have experienced.

After this exercise, remember that if you are to make any changes in waking life because of this symbolic meeting, you will need to consider the effects they may have on yourself and others. Don't rush into changing anything. Give yourself time to reflect on what you have learned, and wait for the next dream or two, which will almost certainly be on the same theme, even though it may not be apparent until you work with the dream. The next dreams you remember may be supportive of the changes you have in mind, or they could show your fears or inhibitions about change. We are all afraid of change, at times. Accept the fear. Perhaps you need to do more work with your fearful side. You could even do the whole exercise all over again, this time taking your fear as the symbol!

Other ways of working with symbols

Another very productive way of working with symbols is to draw, paint, sculpt, or otherwise recreate them. You do not have to be an artist to do this! In fact, traditional art school training will leave you 'schooled' in a way that may impede the spontaneous unconscious flow in this type of dreamwork.

I haven't yet mentioned creative writing, though this has a valuable place in this work, as shown in Part II of this book. However creative, producing the written word as our main focus takes us into our heads to some degree, and is too often the prerogative of the conscious mind. Ruth wrote of her experiences, but only afterwards. She did not create those images and events through her writing, but simply reported them, while keeping the spirit of the dream. We might say that she kept one foot in the unconscious, or in the dream.

Exercise twelve: drawing your symbol

• Try drawing your symbol, using stubby wax crayons, soft pastels, or charcoal rather than pen or pencil, which gives a finer, more precise form of expression. We aim to paint a broad picture here, so if you are using crayons, take the protective paper off, so that you can make a wide stroke using the side of the crayon.

• Choose a large sheet of paper, and have several sheets available in case you want to do more. If you feel that you cannot possibly reproduce your symbol, begin by choosing colours to represent your feelings about it. Then let your arm and wrist move freely, filling the page with sweeps and shapes of colour, without any expectations or control. Just let it flow, remembering there is no right way, so you cannot get it wrong. See the symbol in its dream setting in your mind's eye, and allow it to speak through your drawing. Let it surprise you, and please don't allow your inner critic or censor to judge your artistic efforts as you go.

• When you have finished, take a step back and view what you have created, still bearing the dream in mind. Ask yourself: what does this picture say about your symbol? What can you see there? Does this connect with other dreams, or with waking experience in any way? What might the message of the symbol be? Spend some time quietly reflecting on these questions, letting the process lead you where it will.

• Some people feel more at home with paint, while some prefer using clay to create three-dimensional things. Others may cut out figures and images from magazines to make a collage of their symbol. Begin with whatever feels most comfortable for you, but try out one of the other methods from time to time, working with different dreams. The results may well surprise you!

• Do not show the pictures you create to anyone, certainly not before you've had time to digest what they reveal. Relating to your symbol and your dream in this way is deep and delicate work, which can leave you vulnerable to another's interpretation or dismissal of it. Even our nearest and dearest can make unintentionally wounding comments, not knowing or understanding the inner process that our artwork depicts.

• Keep these pictures, and any written work you produce from your interaction with your dreams, somewhere safe. Sooner or later, you will want to look at them again in relation to a further appearance of the same symbol, and they can be wonderful markers of your progress through dreamwork.

• Start a list of symbols at the back of your dream journal or in a small separate book if you prefer. Go back through all the dreams you've recorded, recognizing the symbols you already have, and then add each new symbol as it occurs. You could experiment with grouping them to see which types of symbol occur most frequently, and how they relate to each other. Each symbol is a jewel, reflecting something of your inner depth and the dazzling awareness of your unconscious mind.

Reflections on chapter five

Working with symbols can be very exciting. They can inspire us, their vibrancy lifting us into an enhanced sense of awareness, or taking us into our inner depth and compassion. You can reflect the mood that the symbol brings in the colours you choose to represent it, and they can carry the feeling into any drawings you may do as follow-up work.

If you have painted a positive symbol, pin it up on the wall, perhaps in your bedroom, or if you are shy of anyone else seeing it, inside a cupboard door where you'll catch a glimpse of it several times each day. This can have a gradual subliminal effect, reminding you of the particular qualities of your symbol and its personal significance. Wearing something of the colour you associate with your symbol helps you hold the energy too.

Stay mindful of your symbol and open to all that it brings. Try not to close down too quickly by thinking that your first understanding of its meaning is the only one. Begin to notice the symbols that are there for you in waking too. Enjoy this new way of connecting with your innermost self and simultaneously gathering new information from the outer world – the collective.

six 6 *Big dreams and archetypes*

'I wake with a delicious sense of floating through the air, circling, spiralling lazily, effortlessly, in the warmth of the sun. There is a rhythmic swish of great wings that may or may not be mine, I am so content that it doesn't seem to matter.

'Then I remember. I was visiting the dragon, my beautiful green dragon, Old Shapeshifter. She was telling me one of the old stories, of the time when the dragons had to 'go to earth', hiding from the new light. She told of how they went into their great sleep. Dragons sleep for thousands of years and as they sleep the leaves fall, new plants grow, the earth rises and covers them. As they forget themselves, lost in their deep slumber, so they become lost in Earth herself, part of the landscape, only occasionally visible and then only to seekers, mystics and children, the ones who haven't yet forgotten how to see.

'I'm filled with excitement as I realize that now, for the first time, she is letting me fly, taking me with her, high up above the fields, woods and hills below. Then, just as suddenly, she is gone and I am alone, making my own circle, soaring and swooping, light and free.

'I hear her call, below me, but she is nowhere to be seen. Looking keenly at the landscape below I see a trickle of smoke that I hadn't noticed before. It seems to be coming from a dark cave on the hillside. Then, as I watch, some way above it the crust of the earth wrinkles and moves and a great glowing yellow eye is revealed! With one mischievous conspiratorial wink it is gone again! Only the remains of a faint plume of smoke trailing from one nostril give any sign that she is there at all. But now I can recognize the ridge of her spine along the top of the hills, the curl of her tail around the river, and the pattern of her beautiful green wings in the folds of the fields.'

I wake up, really awake this time, from the dream within a dream, still caught in the exhilaration of the flight and delight at Shapeshifter's sense of fun as she chose to become a living illustration to her story. I found myself wondering, 'Does the sleeping earthbound dragon revel in her own dreams of flight as she meets me in mine?'

The 'big dream' you have just read came to me several years ago, and formed part of a series of dragon dreams that always left me feeling privileged and empowered. I was struggling with deep disillusionment at the time, reaching for my true inner confidence and feminine authority and, in meeting the dragon, met more of myself. I did not 'work' this dream, but experience it as a resource I can draw upon whenever I choose.

In Christian stories the dragon is the 'loathly worm' that terrorizes people and has to be killed by the heroic knight. But my dreams spoke of a more ancient layer of consciousness, where the dragon is a creature of wisdom guarding the entrance to the cave where the treasure lies. In the great journey along the path of individuation, the 'treasure' is the Self. The fierce dragon is there to carefully scrutinize all who would enter, turning away, frightening off the opportunist, the naive youth, the fool, and the 'sleepwalkers' who are not really conscious of what they are about in everyday life.

Carl Jung had a dream that explains these sedimentary layers in the unconscious: *'I was in a house I did not know which had two storeys. It was "my house". I found myself in the upper storey, where there was a kind of salon furnished with fine old pieces in Rococo style. On the walls hung a number of precious old paintings. I wondered that this should be my house and thought, "Not bad". But then it occurred to me that I did not know what the lower floor looked like. Descending the stairs, I reached the ground floor. There everything was much older and I realized that this part of the house must date from about the fifteenth or sixteenth century. The furnishings were medieval; the floors were of red brick. Everywhere it was rather dark. I went from one room to another, thinking "Now I really must explore the whole house". Beyond it, I discovered a stone stairway that led...into the cellar. Descending again, I found myself in a beautifully vaulted room which looked exceedingly ancient. Examining the walls, I discovered layers of brick among the ordinary stone blocks and chips of brick in the mortar. As soon as I saw this I knew that the walls dated from Roman times.*

'My interest in the house was now intense. I looked more closely at the floor. It was of stone slabs, and in one of these I discovered a ring. When I pulled it, the stone slab lifted and again I saw a stairway of narrow stone steps leading

down into the depths. These, too, I descended, and entered a low cave cut into the rock. Thick dust lay on the floor and in the dust were scattered bones and broken pottery, like remains of a primitive culture. I discovered two human skulls, obviously very old and half-disintegrated.' Then I awoke. (from *Memories, Dreams, Reflections*)

In explaining his understanding of the meaning of this dream Jung went on to say: 'It was plain to me that the house represented a kind of image of the psyche – that is to say, of my then state of consciousness, with hitherto unconscious additions.

'Consciousness was represented by the salon. It had an inhabited atmosphere, in spite of its antiquated style. The ground floor stood for the first level of the unconscious. The deeper I went, the more alien and the darker the scene became. In the cave, I discovered remains of a primitive culture, that is, the world of the primitive man within myself – a world which can scarcely be reached or illuminated by consciousness. The primitive psyche of man borders on the life of the animal soul, just as the caves of prehistoric times were usually inhabited by animals before men laid claim to them.'

This dream gave Jung the foundations for his understanding of the further reaches of the unconscious and his first inkling of a 'collective' beneath the personal psyche, signifying past times and passed stages of consciousness. With further experience he came to realize that these layers in the unconscious were also connected with forms of instinct, which he called archetypes. Each is a kind of matrix or blueprint for the hidden potential within human behaviour, covering the whole spectrum from the highest to the lowest of which we are capable.

This was a truly 'big dream' for Jung which led to him breaking away from his mentor and friend, Sigmund Freud, and eventually establishing his own credentials as a ground-breaking psychologist of great renown. So we might say that 'big dreams' are archetypal dreams, having a numinous, larger-than-life quality that can fill us with wonder or terror. They come to us as we travel through the layers of consciousness in sleep, motivated by the bright source of intelligence at our core that simply wants us to know and grow, remembering who we truly are. These dreams can change our lives.

We don't have to go looking for archetypes; they usually come to us unbidden, and the effect of their energies can be either transformative or destructive. Dreams, which speak the symbolic language of the unconscious, are obviously a very effective channel, but we can also meet archetypal figures in meditation, visualization, or through people we know in waking who, perhaps unknowingly, carry a sub-personality or shadow role for us. At times even a chance encounter can be of truly archetypal dimensions.

The map opposite may help to explain how the impersonal energy of the archetype is mediated to us, whether dreaming or awake, and can intensify our experience. It is by no means the definitive map, but an example of how some of the archetypes may move through the psyche. They may take many and varied forms and, according to our responses to them, move us to different places. Certainly as many have been left out as have been included. We could equally create a map of archetypal symbols or creatures, rather than the figures used in this case. Our own personal map would carry a mixture of all three.

An archetype can resonate with any symbol or sub-personality that carries some trace of an energy similar to its own. This makes that part of us a suitable carrier of its particular force of energy. It then gathers more energy, amplified by the archetype. In this way a good mother sub-personality, acting as a channel for the Great Mother archetype may be represented in dreams as your own mother, grandmother, or other motherly person who has carried some experience of this archetype to you in your lifetime. At a deeper level, the energy may be expressed more symbolically as, for instance, a great tree, a warm dry cave, a fertile landscape, a multi-breasted nurturer, the Virgin Mary or other goddess figure, or Mother Earth herself. Equally the bad mother will symbolically become a spider, snake, whirlpool, devouring beast, a witch, raving madwoman, or suffocating smotherer, when touched by the energy of the Terrible Mother archetype.

The Good Father may be a figure from outer life or a noble lion, a king, a wise old man, a provider, a rock, the sun, God, or Buddha himself. A critical, sarcastic, cold, or brutal father or other authority figure may be shown as a menacing figure wielding a knife, scalpel, or

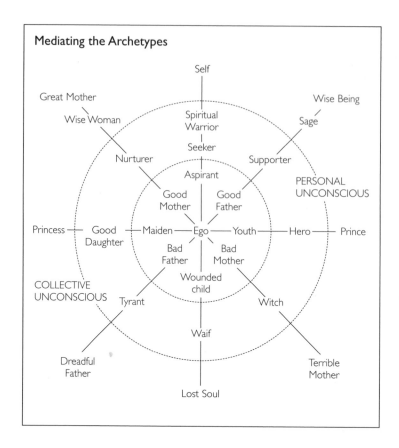

Mediating the Archetypes

Self

Great Mother

Wise Woman

Wise Being

Sage

Spiritual
Warrior

Seeker

Nurturer

Supporter

Aspirant

PERSONAL
UNCONSCIOUS

Good
Mother

Good
Father

Princess — Good — Maiden — Ego — Youth — Hero — Prince
Daughter

Bad
Father

Bad
Mother

COLLECTIVE
UNCONSCIOUS   Tyrant

Wounded
child

Witch

Waif

Dreadful
Father

Terrible
Mother

Lost Soul

axe. Or he may appear as a monster, alien, giant, devouring ogre, wild boar, crocodile or lizard, thunder or lightning bolts – all of which may be images of the archetypal Dreadful Father.

A young woman, survivor of a childhood of almost unremitting sexual and emotional abuse, brought a powerful and disturbing dream which illustrates the horror of the lasting effects of abuse. This long dream begins on a visit to the seaside, with a friend and her children. Susie, one of the young children, goes missing from the funfair on the pier and the dreamer goes to look for her.

She finds her, but as they walk further along to look at something at the end of the pier they are suddenly buffeted by wind and rain, and the wooden boards they are walking on become wet and slippery.

Looking back, she sees to her complete dismay and horror that the pier has either gone, or been submerged by fast-flowing, deep murky water. She scoops Susie up in her arms and tries to walk in the direction of the pavilion on the shore. Disorientated, cold, and almost drowning herself, it is the child she fears for most, knowing that at the very least the little girl will be severely traumatized. The dreamer continues:

'Then I see a sort of black muddy pathway leading to an iron construction of some kind, possibly the underside of a pier. There appear to be other people near or on it. I'm really relieved to have found a way back. I have to jump to avoid sinking in mud and then find myself ankle deep in the muddy water lapping around the edges of mangled iron. I hug Susie close to me and she buries her head in my shoulder.

'I keep her head there with my left arm, holding it firmly but gently as I start walking up some iron steps. They are old and rickety and I don't feel too safe but at least they are a way out of the stinking wet mud at the bottom. I've only gone about three steps up when I see a leg caught in the side of the mangled iron staircase. To begin with I think that someone has fallen, but then I realize that it is the dismembered leg of a woman. It makes me feel sick but I carry on up the steps, holding Susie more closely and tighter to me. Then I see an arm, then a hand – they all have stretched, tight skin, possibly swollen, and blue-grey in colour. A thin, emaciated, haggard-looking woman, possibly in her twenties, filthy dirty and with a black shawl wrapped round her shoulders, passes by me, going down the stairs. She smiles at me and gives me what I can only describe as a beckoning look.

'I turn and follow her and have to pass again the dismembered women's bodies. When we get to the bottom I ask her to show me the way out. She tells me that she has been there for eighteen months and that there is no way out. I find this hard to believe and tell her so. She responds by telling me that she has not always lived in the open under this mangled mess of iron, but that for a long time she lived in a much darker place. She points to a dark, dungeon-type cave that is made up of twisted iron. It looks dark and dismal and has a feel of 'witch' and 'evil' about it.

'I feel that there must be another way out, but the woman insists that there isn't and then points to some people sitting near to where I first came into this iron construction, from the sea. I see men sitting around. Some look as if they are eating, some are still wet from the sea, and others are just staring out to sea as if they are looking for something or somebody. They are all pale and white. One man I notice in particular is grossly overweight, pale, insipid-looking and has an air of arrogance about him.

'The woman says that they arrive every day and yet nobody knows of the place, nor do they know what it is they have got themselves into. Then I see a number of people very similar to the woman I have been talking to, in that they are dirty, tired and worn-looking, surviving, maybe. But they survive by eating the people who get washed up there!

'This terrifies me and I want to get myself and Susie out as quickly as I can, but there is no way out! The woman beckons me with the index finger of her right hand to come into the dark cavernous mangled heap of iron. I can't. It is too dangerous. I have to protect Susie, as well as myself. We both have to get out of here. This woman reminds me of a witch and I do not want to be anywhere near her. I just feel…total panic.'

The dream ended here, the dreamer left considering her options. Should she go into the awful iron hole of the witch? Or go up the staircase and risk being dismembered? To try to get back into the sea, even at the risk of drowning, seems preferable. At least she and Susie would die together. But she would have to negotiate the people sitting at the edge and they might take Susie and eat her!

This terrifying archetypal nightmare seems to offer no solutions or healing, no hope. It symbolizes the desperation and terror felt by those who have been severely abused. The dream setting moves from a pier – a structure which bridges sea and shore, where families go to have fun – to a sinister, dark, watery environment, not subterranean, but just a little way below everyday conscious awareness. Yet those on the pier are oblivious to it. This symbolizes part of the predicament of the abused child when the family remains unaware, or unconsciously chooses to remain in collusive denial.

The dream brings in the sub-personality of the lost child, who may symbolize the splitting off of part of the personality, which occurs in young children who have been cruelly violated and traumatized. There is also the young woman who has adapted in order to become a survivor, but endures a life of misery and deprivation at the edge of life, the border between conscious and unconscious. The dreamer perceives her as a witch, and here is the Dark Mother archetype, mediated by the sub-personality of the young woman. The gross fat man, the abuser, bloated through feeding off little children, symbolizes the Negative Masculine archetype. We might see the dreamer and child symbolically caught here, between Dreadful Father and Terrible Mother.

But it is the image of the hole, or cave and the scene of dismemberment as possibly the only way out that take us to an altogether different level. The witch wanted the dreamer to follow her into the hole, or cave. In primitive mythology the cave was the place of women; in Mexico 'The Western hole into which the sun descends is the archetypal womb of death, destroying what has been born.' For the Aztecs, the hole represents, 'The primeval home where humankind once crawled from the primordial hole of the earth.' (Both of these descriptions are taken from Erich Neumann's *The Great Mother*.) Here, in this symbol, we find the Death and Rebirth archetype, which emphasizes the gravity of the dreamer's situation.

Dismemberment, along with blood sacrifice, belongs to the fertility ritual of another archetype, the Great Mother. Before she gained her corn goddess, Earth Mother identity, the Mother in her terrible aspect was seen as water, as were both the night and the unconscious. If angered, she might flood the earth. In ancient Aztec ritual, the Snake Woman goddess was worshipped with blood sacrifice so that she would bring fertility to the land. In early Mexican and some Egyptian traditions this Terrible Mother had to be offered sacrifices, which often took the form of decapitation and dismemberment, to avert the danger of flood. In some cultures the dismembered remains were placed in the fields to rot, to renew the earth's fertility.

This bloody, watery aspect of the Terrible Mother generated the myth of the great Serpent or Dragon of darkness that rises at night and has to be killed each day by the Hero, another archetype, so that the land is not flooded. Here is the mythical Hero's journey to the underworld, a journey of transformation and rebirth. The sickle crescent of the moon is sometimes seen as the Hero's weapon, with which each day the Mother herself is dismembered, becoming the source of new life. Here again we encounter the Death and Rebirth archetype, and also the fertility of the Great Mother.

The dreamer, a modern young woman, knew nothing of such mythologies or symbolism, yet her Dream Maker was able to access these deep and primitive levels of the collective unconscious, using the dream to give a clear and unforgettable picture of the depth of suffering within her psyche. No one would choose dismemberment, but sometimes it is the only way through to healing, a taking apart of the old psychological constructs, breaking down the sense of identity, using this psychic 'body' to fertilize the new growth of the being.

Of course, not all 'big dreams' are of such a sobering nature. The collective is the home of the gods; saints and angels as well as demons abound here, along with the wonderful creatures of myth and legend. It is the place these stories come from, and a wellspring of creative inspiration of all kinds. When we journey to this place we are reminded of those who have passed before, and we begin to learn that not only is there a map, but others have followed it, explored the terrain, found what they needed to help them through, and survived! In a sense we can come to realize that we are not alone, and there is great comfort in this.

The power of archetypes

We must be especially careful when working with archetypal energies and images. The merest touch of any of them is enough. Each one carries a pure force of energy, so powerful that were we to come too close, look too directly at it, it would blow us away. Because it is impersonal, it has no concern or respect for the individual. Unlike the ego, it cannot reflect upon itself, it just is.

When we meet an archetype in dreams, stories, or as a larger-than-life figure in waking, there is always a strong emotional reaction and the one common response is a feeling of awe, be it experienced as awesomeness or awfulness.

AWESOME_____ AWE _____AWFUL
(Superhuman)   (Humility)   (Sub-human)

Along this scale we may find spiritual enlightenment or abject terror, depending on the nature of the archetype. It may intensify our experience, deepen our awareness, leave us feeling humble and privileged – but we must not identify with it. That is the way of madness! Our little ego cannot begin to contain such overwhelming forces of energy and when we become inflated by the presence of such energies, positive or negative, we lose all sense of perspective and true sense of self.

Nowhere is this more obvious than when we see someone over-reaching themselves and then watch them tumble and fall when their endeavours fail, or they are found out as they attempt to deceive others as well as themselves. I am reminded of the recent real-life case of a young man I'll call the Englishman, who worked as a trader for a well known bank in Singapore. He was a terrific high flyer, and had huge success, bringing the bank immense profits, winning respect, and great acclaim. He was given almost total power and control. A superhuman expectation was placed on him, perhaps because he had already accepted it for himself.

But behind the boy wonder sub-personality lurked another, a devious Trickster. Feeling under great pressure to continually excel, he began to make illegal transactions, taking greater and greater risks with the bank's money, losing millions of dollars, and disguising his increasing losses in a hidden account. When they were too great to maintain the deception, he was discovered, and the bank was ruined. The bank lost a great deal of money and credibility, many people lost their jobs, even more lost their investments, and the Englishman was sent to prison in Singapore.

This story has epic proportions and harks back to the ancient Greek myth of Icarus, whose father, Daedalus, was a man of great genius and ingenuity. Daedalus had designed the labyrinth to help King Minos contain the terrible Minotaur, half-bull, half-man. When Theseus killed the Minotaur, Daedalus – with his unique knowledge of the plan of the labyrinth – helped the goddess Ariadne to save Theseus by giving him a ball of thread with which he was able to find his way out. For this act of treachery, Minos imprisoned Daedelus and his son Icarus.

But Daedelus was a wily and clever inventor with more than a touch of the Trickster archetype about him. He created fabulous wings of wax, so that they could both fly to freedom. Then he gave one set to Icarus, with the warning, 'Take care not to fly too high, nor too close to the sun.'

The wings gave Icarus the power of flight, an archetypal power, since mere men cannot fly. But Icarus was young and intoxicated by this sudden freedom and the joy of flight. He 'forgot himself', beginning to believe that he really was superhuman. Higher and higher he swooped, so high in fact that he got too close to the heat of the sun, which melted his waxen wings. He crashed down into the sea, where he died.

The Englishman seemed to combine these elements of the Trickster and the Flying Boy in his dealings at the bank. The Flying Boy or Peter Pan figure is not one to trust with such responsibilities. He is usually full of bravado and more gullible than he thinks. He can easily be flattered into an alliance with the Trickster. Living in the grip of such an archetype, he knows no conscience. Recognizing neither normal, grounded boundaries and limitations nor his own human vulnerability, he will inevitably fly too high and 'get his wings burnt'.

When the high flyer is caught breaking the law, society will be outraged and punish him severely as he comes crashing down. If he survives this punishment, he has a chance to wake up, recognize his weaknesses, and work to achieve a more honourable way of life. But often these 'fallen boys' come close to death as a result. Certainly their life has to change if they are to go on.

This is a modern tale, but one with clear links into the ancient past. When the archetype is present, whether for Icarus or the Englishman, human behaviour doesn't change very much, does it? Perhaps the gods are closer than we realize!

In jail, which was in itself a nightmare situation for this urbane and materialistic man, the Englishman developed cancer. He moved from being caught by one archetype into having to surrender total control of his life to another, the Singaporean penal system. Even on leaving prison he carries the possible death sentence of his illness. Is this not a truly tragic story of archetypal 'possession'?

You may have noticed a common theme of sacrifice in these dreams and other-worldly stories. The dragon sacrificed flight so that it could hide and survive in the world of men. In Jung's life, after he'd understood the meaning of his dream, he had to let go of his admiration for Freud, suffering necessary disillusion, in order to find his own way. The young witch-woman, who had as a child been sacrificed to the abuser's lust, chose a half-life in the twilight world under the wrecked pier, unable to find her way back to a normal life. When Daedelus helped Ariadne and Theseus, he must have known that he ran the risk of losing his freedom but he was unaware that he also placed his son's life in jeopardy. Had Icarus listened to his father's warning when he gained his wings, he need not have died. If those in thrall to the superhuman dimensions of the Englishman's success had stopped to question, the bank might not have fallen.

Sacrifice is always a difficult concept to accept, but in meeting the archetype, making the mythic journey, the ego must make sacrifices. When we encounter the archetypes, the ego cannot go it alone. It needs all the help it can get and may have to let go of its cherished ambitions and life plan. A crisis of this kind feels terrible, almost like death itself. It is in fact a 'little death'; the necessary death of the ego as it surrenders to the Self.

When we stop struggling to live the life we expect, recognize the need for change, and just let go to what comes, there can be great relief. Suddenly everything is simple, we seem to have more time, fewer attachments, and less pressure. Here's an example from a dreamer who has reached this state of acceptance.

'I'm walking alone, across sand dunes by the ocean. I pick up a stick and use it to try to write my name in the soft dry sand, but it's impossible. The side of the dune slips down and obscures it as fast as I write. Climbing a dune, I shout

my name out loud, but the breeze and the cries of the gulls catch it and carry it away. Going down to the shoreline, I inscribe my name with a flourish in the wet sand. Now it can be clearly seen! But in no time at all, little wavelets wash over it and it is gone. Letting go to inevitability, I lie down at the water's edge and patiently await the incoming tide.'

Archetypal situations

At some point in our lives, most of us meet an archetype through a situation we cannot control. Accident, illness, natural disasters, and war are all great levellers, indiscriminately affecting large sections of the community. The archetypes are also present when we collectively share in such events as coronations, birth, christenings, first communions, weddings, and funerals. In every culture these occasions have become ritualized as people come together to recognize, honour, witness, celebrate, or grieve.

Ceremony and ritual form an integral part of the way that the archetypes are mediated to us. It is usual for the clergy to officiate, the priest becoming a living channel for the archetypal energies, his spiritual training enabling him to take the lead in showing respect and deference to them. Once it would have been the shaman, witch doctor, tribal chief, wise woman, or healer who fulfilled this role.

Nowadays for many in the West, the traditional church seems to have lost its vitality and more and more people are looking to gurus or charismatics for spiritual leadership and vision. There is a resurgence of interest in shamanism, and some individuals are finding faith and trust in their own inner wisdom. It is not uncommon for couples to have a registry office wedding, followed by a celebration that includes a second, sacred ceremony without clergy officiating, which has been planned with careful thought and mutual respect.

Ceremony honours the rites of passage as we move from one stage of life to another. It 'sets the seal' on an archetypal event, providing a safe and respectful container. Such rituals mark the thresholds of an initiation. Without a funeral or burial service, grief may feel unending. Without due ceremony, a wedding may not feel blessed. In England, when the monarch dies, the new king or queen is immediately proclaimed, but it is the coronation that dignifies and concretizes the occasion.

When you find any of these situations or occasions in your dreams, this is the Dream Maker telling you that the archetype is present, that it is time for a new phase to be ushered in, or for your current experience to be recognized and validated by some kind of ceremony.

In dream workshops I am continually in awe of the wisdom of people when they realize they have reached such a place. Held within their inner process by the container and energies of the workshop, they create their own rituals when the time is right, instinctively knowing just what they need. Members of the group will usually be invited along to witness what is being given up or brought into being, and there is great healing here.

Balancing the archetypes

We've already featured some of the darker archetypes in this chapter. Let's now do what we need to do when their energies are present: a little balancing. There are polarities in these energies. When we are struggling under the effects of a negative archetype, we need to invite in its opposite. This, of course, requires a good understanding of your inner process first of all.

We cannot control or manipulate the archetypes. As I have said, they simply are what they are. Because by their very nature they are impersonal, we cannot easily relate directly to them and our little ego can feel defeated by their omnipotent presence. We have to meet like with like, balance one archetypal energy with its equal and opposite energy. A good way to do this is to take the same approach as the archetypes. They come to us through the energy of symbol or an appropriate sub-personality.

So if, for example, the children in your dreams have led you into working with your wounded inner child, you may be at a loss as to how to help and comfort him or her. Perhaps you lack a good role model for mothering yourself. Or you may find, at first, that you feel angry and rejecting of this unhappy or troubled child with its cargo of shame and pain. Yet something needs to be done.

What you can do is find within you a 'good enough' mother figure. She doesn't have to be perfect but will need to be able to feel compassion or tenderness, so that she can empathize with your 'child's' pain. If you feel that this is beyond you, you might look to someone you know in waking who has these qualities and let that person act as a symbol for you for the time being. Sometimes a grandmother fulfils this role well, in dreams, inner, and outer life. Or perhaps a neighbour or friend you've admired for the way they parent their children. Having found a suitable figure, you can symbolically, in your imagination, let this good enough mother be with your inner child and learn from seeing how she comforts her. Then you can invite in the archetype of the Great Mother, or Goddess, to nurture them both.

If your child is always alone, sad and isolated in dreams, remember that you also have within you a Wondrous Child, who knows how to play and befriend. Maybe your 'child' needs a playmate every bit as much as a mother. Introduce your wounded little one to this wondrous child, the one for whom life sparkles with magic, wonder, and awesome possibility. Now let them become playmates, blessed by the Angel of Companionship. For every demon, you can be sure there will also be an angel. If you find you are out of balance and have too strong a Masculine energy, invite in the Feminine, regardless of your gender. If you are overwhelmed by too much of the negative Dark Feminine, call in a Hero to fight your corner. (Never would a rescuing Hero have been more welcome than in the earlier 'pier' dream, although when your faith has been all but destroyed, it may be the Spiritual Warrior who is most needed.)

When psychic Death feels close, remember that Rebirth is possible and that there are times when it is wiser to surrender than to fight. For, without the death of the old way, we cannot create the psychic space needed for birth and renewal.

Exercise thirteen: invoking an archetype

In this exercise I will stay with the mother/child example, but you can of course adapt it to suit any other sub-personality and archetype. The qualities and type of energy needed will differ accordingly, so you will need to give some thought to this first. We must always be careful what we wish for, so be sure to ground yourself and your process securely, giving careful consideration to what you are about. The key word here is balance, not revenge, retribution, judgement, or aggrandisement.

• Knowing the issues you are working with, find a quiet time for this exercise. To move your energies and attitude into a suitably mindful and respectful frame of mind for a meeting with an archetype, I suggest you thoughtfully create a sacred space before you begin. Light a candle, dedicating it to the sub-personality involved. Bring in something which is symbolic of that part of you, as a reminder, a token of their qualities and energy. You may also want to place here a symbol or talisman which carries healing energy for you and may help you hold your centre. This might be a crystal, a special stone, flower, or a small object which holds value for you.

• Now sit quietly in your sacred space, turning your attention first to the figure whom you feel may be able to help. Begin to visualize this person clearly, perhaps in the setting of a dream, or in some appropriate familiar place. When you can see them clearly, welcome them and let them know that you are here to ask for their help. Explain the situation to this person – in this case the good enough mother and ask if she is willing to help you to look after your inner child. Ask how much she feels able to do and let her know that it won't be forever. That you want to learn from her so that you can take on this task for yourself. If she agrees, you are ready to move on to the next stage of the exercise. If she feels she cannot help you, you will need to find another figure, and leave the rest of this exercise for later. Maybe you could invite this new suitable figure to come to you in a dream.

• If she is willing, ask her to come with you now to meet your inner child, but make sure that she stays on the sidelines until you have had a chance to meet with the child and explain what is about to happen. We need to be just as respectful towards a child, any child, as we do to the most imposing of adults!

• Now visualize your wounded child, seeing her in a place that is comfortable for her to be in. You are going to her, in her place, not asking her to come to you at this stage. Greet her sensitively and let her know that even though you yourself may not yet be in a position to offer as much help to her as you would like, you have brought someone with you who wants to get to know her and look after her.

• Give your child time to adjust to this concept before moving on to invite the good enough mother in, then step back and let them take the first tentative steps towards getting to know each other. Watch and wait, seeing how the good enough mother does it, and noting how the child responds to this new approach.

• When you feel they have established a good rapport, quietly invite in the Great Mother, or Goddess to be with them, to nurture and support them both. Again, just watch and wait and see if this changes anything in the nature of their relationship. A figure symbolizing the archetype may appear and talk with them, or simply watch over them. There may be some subtle change of energy, or it may seem that nothing happens, but just trust that your call will be heard and answered, perhaps not obviously and immediately, but a response will come.

• Take your cues from what is happening in your visualization and, when the moment feels right, ask if there is anything they need from you. Only agree to do what truly feels possible, but remember that you do have an important role here. After all, you are the one who has done the work up to now, and brought them all together. You and you alone hold the awareness and responsibility for this process as it is.

• When the time feels right to bring the meeting to an end, thank everyone for being with you in this way and say your goodbyes. Then give yourself time to let the images go and return your awareness to the room you are in. Make sure you are fully back in your body by stretching and moving around a little. You may like to make a warm drink to ground yourself more securely before sitting to write what you have experienced in your journal.

Once you have done this dreamwork exercise you will find it easy to touch in to the good enough mother and your inner child whenever you wish, to see how their relationship is growing in trust and love, and to learn from this.

Of course, if you find that you are able to mother your wounded child yourself, then you can simply invite in the archetype to support you in this task, without the need for a sub-personality to mediate the energy for you.

Continuing the journey

We can ask these balancing energies to come to us in our dreams – try affirming your intent for three consecutive nights, then wait for a few days and see what comes. Sometimes they will already be there, but unrecognized, so the dreams may once more present symbols, characters, or situations that seem familiar to you, challenging you to take a fresh look.

Mostly we dream of symbols and archetypes within our own culture, but not always. Anna, a British girl living in London decided to incubate a dream while working with the Shadow archetype. Before going to sleep, she asked the following questions: 'What do you want from me, Shadow? How can I help you in my conscious, waking life? What do you need and desire?' That night she dreamed:

'*We arrive at a place, I think it's Africa or India. Anyway we have to follow the river up alongside the length of Belgium to get to a place called Ashtar (Ishtar?), where there is a temple or mosque which has been the scene of heavy fighting.*

'*We get to the mesquita with hardly any effort, although I had expected it to take days. We are allowed in to the temple (I thought maybe we wouldn't be, being women and perhaps not suitably attired; in other words, showing too much flesh), and to my surprise it feels very much like a Catholic church, but not sombre or over-the-top in décor. This church is light and airy; there is more room inside than I thought. There's a side room which is shaped like an octagon or polygon and it has a huge picture of a mother and child (but not à la Botticelli, in the religious style). I stay there and meditate for a while then I come out and say, "This mesquita is just like a Catholic church".*

'*We are eating slices of fruit – it must be red. Watermelon, or raspberries, or red pears. The redness of the fruit is important. By now we are just down the road from Mary Evans' house, Rossville. Maybe the church is our local in Ireland, our Lady of Perpetual Succour.*'

'On waking it's very clear that I should worship at the temple of the Feminine, and honour the Spirit. Maybe go back to childhood, to Mary's school and the freedom of that experience? But it wasn't really free, because mummy taught the big ones there!'

The influence of the collective unconscious is clearly at work in this dream. Anna had never heard of the great Assyro–Babylonian Goddess Ishtar, goddess of the morn and goddess of the evening. She was the divine personification of the planet Venus and therefore goddess of love, though in some aspects she was also known as a warrior goddess. Intrigued by the name, Anna looked it up and understood that the dream described a journey into the deep Feminine, going beyond the familiar landmarks of her own culture, her school in Ireland, the Catholic church, Belgium. She followed the Feminine symbol of the river into what she thought was Africa or India, to visit the temple of an ancient culture and begin to learn another way of the Feminine. Interesting, since the question was asked of the Shadow.

Anna was fortunate in that her dream gave her the name of the goddess so she was able to find out about her. I have often had people bring dreams of being in a far distant place looking at a symbol or geometric pattern or a city which they knew was of significance and which felt to be really ancient. Yet on waking they have had so little to go on they have not been able to place what they found either historically or geographically. Even so, they have sensed that something new – old–new – was being brought into consciousness with some purpose which was relevant to their current process.

Sometimes, in our darkest hour, a balancing archetype will come to us spontaneously, already complete. It may appear as a personally meaningful healing symbol, which could be a crystal, an angel, a tree, a flower, an animal, a tranquil pool or other watery image; a bird, a warm fire, or a loving person. The variations are endless, depending on the symbolic images and energy of each person's inner journey. It may take the form of a Being of Light, who bathes us in radiant love and compassion for a timeless moment that feels as if it stretches into infinity. This is always a transformative encounter, sometimes accompanied by a telepathically received 'voice' that speaks of our difficulties and offers guidance.

In a near-death experience this Being of Light may take you on a journey into the light, sometimes including a review of your life and offering you the choice to stay or return. Such 'travellers' return altered, spiritually enriched, with a new awareness and stronger sense of Self. Life is never quite the same for them again.

At other times, this guidance may simply come as a small voice whispering in your ear, or through another human being who carries some of the same qualities as the Angel, offering unsolicited love and assistance.

Try to stay mindful of the possibilities for transformation and healing when the archetypes are present. Even at their most awful, the experiences of deprivation and suffering they bring may be seen eventually as great gifts. They compel us to change something we may have felt unable to contemplate, and cause us to grow rather than stagnate or become complacent.

If you feel overwhelmed by such powerful forces it might be a good idea to seek professional help for a while. Someone who works with transpersonal skills may be able to meet you on this level, to help you to make sense of what is happening or support you in learning to accept the unavoidable. Or perhaps they will recognize the need for the Spiritual Warrior, and help to call this up within you, so that you can fight and overcome your inner demons. Here is the dream of someone who did this herself:

She writes, 'I woke up with this 'big dream' at my fingertips…

'I'm in an old, dark house with old–young people. We live outside of society, hidden in the dark, and separate. We live like this to survive. There is violence and pain in this separation that causes some kind of caving in and sickness in the people as they struggle to keep the flame of the old ways awake, as they struggle to hold the thinning thread of the old ways. It gets darker.

'Something happens. Men from the other world are coming to hunt us out, to beat us out into the light, into the open where we will be burnt and destroyed by the violence of their light.

'The old–young people gather themselves. They are dirty and tired and full of hope, full of knowing that they must travel with their drumbeat, with their knowing of the old ways, with the music emerging; that they must travel deeper into the forest. Like refugees, like hopeful but dirty guerrillas of this war, they get into a kind of lorry or caravan. I get in too, but only to say goodbye to them. I long for it to be my way, to go with them, but I cannot pretend that it is. They are younger and older than me, and I must stay.

'I must stay on the topside world and hide in the light so that
I will not be burnt. I must hide by being visible so that I will be seen and, in
that, I will not be seen. So, I will stay hidden. I must find a way. A lot depends
on it. That I find a way to hold deep in my heart, to hold in my belly, in the
wild dark forest of me, the other end of the thread of the old–young people, the
dreaming of them that is the dream of Earth herself. That, as they travel deeper,
away from the light, I must stay on the surface holding the thread. A lot depends
on this – that I stay with the beat of their music as they travel deeper, that I stay
open to the pulse of their music which is the pulse of the Earth herself. So that
there are still places open for us, for those to hear her call home, so there are still
gateways, oracles, and listening wells.

'And I know it will be lonely when they go, yet strangely I know also that
they are not my tribe. They also know this. We do not pretend. They go. I turn
to face the world, and I am ready.'

(Still within the dream.) 'Now after this dream is done, I know that I will
not be alone. I must find the others who stand holding these threads that lead
back to the Mother. Not so that I may cling to them. No, that cannot be any
more. It is so that I can know that I do not stand in this pulse alone, nor they –
this is important. It is so that we may weave an invisible gossamer web across
the topside to hold us in our holding, to send breath across the web, to the world,
for all her people.'

The dreamer had already worked with her dreams for some time
before experiencing this one. It's truly awesome, isn't it? Don't worry if
you don't understand – it's not your dream or process! You can be sure,
though, that when archetypal energies enter your dreams, they will
bring a message of personal, as well as universal, significance.

Reflections on chapter six

Working with archetypes offers such possibilities and often brings a
sense of expansion, dissolving old boundaries to understanding and
giving a clearer vision. Perhaps a window opens in your mind, helping
you to see something familiar in a new light.

We cannot change the archetypes but we can respond to their
appearance in our dreams. If you become aware of the archetypal
energies at work in your life and this disturbs you, use the balancing

exercise. Work through an appropriate sub-personality rather than trying to take on an archetype directly and always invite in help and support. If you have an inspirational archetypal dream, you may simply want to hold it in your heart as a source of strength, hope, and renewal.

Give yourself time to contemplate the forces and events that have directed your life's journey so far. Recognize the choices you have made and the moments where the forces of fate have intervened. What has inspired you? Who has brought great gifts? Where have you been severely tested? How did you cope? What brought you through? What can you willingly let go of now, and what do you need as you continue on your way? What makes your heart sing?

Take a little time to meditate, to open up to the new energy you would like to invite in to your life. Welcome it in, then let it be, and simply wait and see.

Reflections at the end of Part I

This is a good time to pause, reflect on what you have learned and check out how your dreamwork is going.

Have you done all of the exercises, more than once, using different dreams each time? Even experienced dreamworkers, when doing a review of this kind, will find that they favoured or overused one technique at the expense of another. Resolve to try again the ones you didn't get on too well with the first time around. There may be some resistance here – and behind that, a gift!

Spend some time looking back over Part I of the book to remind yourself of the exercises and practical suggestions you have covered during this part of your dream journey. Don't worry or feel that you've failed if you don't think you have achieved many of these things. This book is only a beginning. Give yourself time; you are on your way. We all need to work at our own pace, and you may realize during this review that you have done more than you think.

part **II** *Finding your path through story*

part II *Introduction*

We are ready now to move to a different level of the work. I feel that the last chapter on archetypes has already paved the way. Working with archetypes is different. You can't impose a structure but have to 'feel your way' into what is already there. Following these 'big dreams' and linking the messages they bring leads us into an almost mythical progression, a developing story – your story!

All dreams tell a story. There is the cameo of the dream itself, which is part of a larger picture as dream succeeds dream and we grow in understanding and self-realization. I usually ask people starting my dreamwork courses to bring their earliest remembered dream. When we have the skills to open up this dream, we often find the seeds of the life process! We find that the essential story of that first dream is not so different from their most recent when they begin dreamwork. The characters and setting may have changed, but the underlying issues and conflicts may be painfully familiar and the archetypes are usually the same.

If we continue to 'sleepwalk' through life, these patterns will remain unchanged until something happens to 'wake us up'– an illness, accident, bereavement, or other major loss. But we don't have to wait, unprepared, for the unexpected and often unwelcome wake up call. Of course such things happen from time to time when the Fates take a hand. These are archetypal figures from Greek mythology – Clotho, Lachesis, and Atropho – three old hags who spin, weave, and cut the cloth of life. We cannot avoid them; their work is in the patterning of our lives. However, if we can choose to go to meet them with open eyes and arms, we are better able to receive and wear the cloth they've fashioned for us.

Relating to our dream life can help to equip us for this, showing us how we are making our journey, who we choose to travel with, and how we respond or react to these travelling companions and the situations we find ourselves in. The Dream Maker can show us where the current path may lead and give us the skills, tools, and sensitivity to act in ways that are more true to ourselves.

On the way, we begin to recognize that we are indeed part of a living story. As we weave together messages from our dreams and our waking experiences, we can translate our knowledge into an understanding of plot, characters, events, and the forces that have governed or guided our lives. This is the stuff of fairy tale, myth, and legend. Here we are in the midst of it – living it!

We are moving now from the tools and mechanics of dreamwork into more of a sense of the mystery not just of our dreams, but of the whole of life. Looking back through your dreams will help you to begin to identify your own story. Quite probably you will find yourself recognizing similarities in traditional stories, especially fairy tales. What was your favourite fairy tale as a child? Which character do you identify with? Try to really remember this story for a moment or two. Better still, reread it if you can.

Think about the story, comparing it with your experiences in life. Are there any similarities? What if everything in the story were true on two levels; inner as well as outer? What if it is really part waking experience and part dream? The wicked stepmother of the fairy tale may be an actual unloving stepmother brought into the family by your father. It may be that her behaviour had such a powerful effect that she has become archetypalized, no longer just unkind and insensitive but archetypally Wicked too.

Many modern, successful women have an inner Cinderella figure that they feel ashamed of, hidden away and forgotten within. As with the king in the fairy tales, who was never there to protect his children, there are now too many absent fathers. Single mothers juggle work and family responsibilities, having to be both parents, with no time, energy, or opportunity to live the life of their princess.

And where are the princes and heroes? In the old stories, when the Wicked Witch, as possessive, dark mother, turned them into frogs, they became cold-blooded, unfeeling, disempowered travesties of themselves. Or, touched by the Snow Queen, symbol of the negative animus, they were 'turned to stone'. Thankfully, nowadays more men are learning to be unashamedly in touch with their feelings. It is no longer so much the Dark Feminine but the more mundane practicalities which divest men of their nobility. For all but a few, the need to survive in a material world overwhelms the need for great adventure. So what of the Wild Man and Wild Woman, the Wandering Poet, and the Gypsy Girl? How often do they dance naked beneath the moon, sit and dream by the river, play and make passionate love in wild places? Sometimes, in our dreams, they do!

We need these inspiring dreams to stir our souls. They remind us of our fiery or romantic nature, of the need to be a little crazy sometimes. How long is it since you danced in the rain, slept beneath the stars, wandered through the woods for hours following the deer, or laughed until you cried?

When we combine the world of our dreams with waking life, we find our story. All of it, the longing and the pain, the magic moments, and the delight. That which we've lived to the full, and the aspects of ourselves which are still waiting for a life. Our story will show the patterns which caught and held us as a child, and which still hold sway over us to this day. It will show how we've coped, what we've created and co-created, as well as what we've undone.

Telling your own story is the next thing I am going to ask you to do. You may find that thought alarming. Don't worry, you don't have to be a writer to do it, you can't get it wrong, and you'll certainly learn a great deal from the experience. You may want to tell the whole of your life story chronologically, from birth to the present day. Or you may find it easier to simply hold the focus of the story that has unfolded in the pages of your journal as you've read this book. In fact, you've already written a lot as you've worked through Part I, writing out your dreams, trying the various exercises, and noting insights, feelings, and realizations along the way.

You've already tried moving into observer mode, to get a new perspective on a dream, viewing it as if it were a movie or play. It's a small step from there into becoming a narrator, or storyteller. As we relate our story, parts of the jigsaw fall into place. We begin to recognize that we have feelings and needs that clearly call out to be met. We find our resources, recognizing where we've used them effectively and the progress we've made. We can begin to identify our strengths and weaknesses, to see where we've misjudged people and events, to forgive ourselves and others, so that we can move on.

To help you to see yourself and your life in this way, Part II of this book presents the stories written by two dreamworkers on my course. These were ordinary people, new to creative writing, who balked at the task at first, feeling they couldn't possibly do it. But when they sat with their dream journals and began to realize what rich material they had, they were able to make a start. When you give yourself to the task in this way, the story usually flows. Sometimes it's hard to know when to stop!

The first story was written by Jim (I have changed only his name), an engineer in his mid-fifties. Jim had never written anything like this before, and as the deadline approached he was dismayed to find his story just wasn't coming. In the end, the day before the storytelling weekend, Jim took a day off work to get to grips with this unfamiliar challenge. He sat to meditate first to clear his mind, knowing that he couldn't write in a panic. Then he started writing and was amazed by the result, because the story just wrote itself! He told me, 'I didn't think it was me writing it! Well, it was definitely me – and yet it wasn't!'

This is a fairly common experience, for when we manage to 'get out of our own way', as Jim did by meditating, our inner wisdom and creative juices can flow as the material springs, almost complete, straight out of the repository of the unconscious. Jim called his story *The Inheritance*.

The second story – *The Rose and the Key* – was written by Helen, an astrologer in her late thirties. She too was new to creative writing of this kind, and as you read of her experiences while she was on our training course, all of which became part of her story, you may wonder that she had the time or energy to write at all. Like Jim, Helen is not a writer, and didn't realize that she had the capacity, talent, or skill to relate her personal story in such a creative way. It is a very beautiful and moving story and I'm sure you will enjoy it.

seven / *Jim's story*

The Inheritance

There was once a dark castle called Sleep. In it dwelt a wicked queen and her stepson. The boy was heir to an inheritance, the nature of which had been kept from him by the queen, who was jealous of him and wanted to possess him, and kept him in a tower, under a spell, in deep sleep.

One day, a bird alighted on the windowsill of the lad's chamber and sang so loudly that he stirred in his sleep and asked, 'What is that?'

'Lie-a-bed, lie-a-bed, lie-a-bed!' shrieked the bird. 'Do you intend to stay under your stepmother's spell for ever?'

'Go away,' the boy said, and turned over.

'Lie-a-bed, lie-a-bed,' shrieked the bird again and flew off.

The boy tried to go to sleep again, but could not. Something was in the room, something that disrupted his stepmother's spell and drew him to it. Sitting up, he saw a single white feather. When he picked it up, he saw written on it, 'Your journey is begun. Go east. When you need me, whistle three times'.

His stepmother, sensing the disruption of her spell, came to his room. Still drowsy, he allowed her to hold him on the bed and murmur to him. 'Mummy's child; go to sleep; be mine; never wake; go to sleep, sleep, sleep,' but the feather in his hand seemed to cry at him, 'Lie-a-bed, lie-a-bed,' and with mounting terror he suddenly leapt out of her grasp, through the open door, and to his freedom.

One of his mother's councillors, the judge, had seen him go and hastened after him. 'Where are you going?' he asked.

'East,' said the boy, who had not recognized him.

'Then I will travel with you,' said the judge.

As they walked, the boy told him his story and the judge rebuked him, saying, 'How could you be so ungrateful to such a kind unselfish mother? Aren't you ashamed?'

He advised the lad that, to redeem himself (for he was now thoroughly ashamed), he must marry the first woman he met in the city of the east. But the judge had secretly sent a message to the queen, telling her where they were headed.

In the east the land was white. He encountered fur-clad, booted men, women with high cheekbones and inward-looking eyes, sonorous singing in the churches, great bells sending their reverberations over city and country.

Here he learned to understand melody and taught himself to play the flute. But it was not long before he met a beautiful woman and, mindful of his shame, he wooed her and married her to redeem his guilt. Imagine his horror, therefore, when as soon as he had her alone, she unmasked herself and revealed herself to be none other than his stepmother! At once he fell into a trance again and she, mounting his back and hanging on with two hands and two feet, cried, 'Now I have you! Now I have you! You must sleepwalk where I send you and carry me forever!'

And for twenty one years he did just that, scarcely awake at all, until one day his sleep was punctuated by a cry, 'Lazybones, lazybones! Do you intend to stay under the spell of your stepmother forever?'

With a mighty effort he threw himself to the ground and rolled over, breaking his stepmother's grasp. Leaping to his feet, he whistled three times. The bird flew low over him, crying 'Go south, go south!' So he fled, taking his flute, leaving his stepmother stricken where she fell.

Once again, as he travelled, he was counselled by a travelling companion, who reproached him for his harsh treatment of his stepmother. The judge, for it was he, said that to redeem himself he had to enter the service of a great lady in the city of the south. But he sent a message to the queen, telling her where they were. The young man heeded the judge's advice, telling himself he would never again make a mistake such as the last one.

In the south the land was red: red rock, red earth in which the olives and oranges and vines sought sparse nourishment. The city had water for streets, wherein were reflected palaces and churches, bridges, and hovels. The boat men sang songs of love and passion to the sound of the mandolin, so he bought himself one and taught himself harmony. Mindful of his remorse, the young man sought out the great lady and with scarcely any sense of danger, offered his services. She put him in livery and, as soon as he had done up the last button, he saw her for who she was, for it was his stepmother once again. He fell into a deep trance and she rode him, hanging on by two hands and one foot. 'Now I have you! Now I have you! You must sleepwalk where I send you and carry me forever!'

And so for seven years he carried her, until one day he heard the cry, 'Slothful, slothful! Do you intend to stay under your stepmother's spell forever?'

With a cry, he leaped into the canal, so that his stepmother loosed her hold for fear of drowning. Swimming to the edge, he whistled three times. 'Where now?' he asked.

'Go west, go west!' cried the bird.

So, taking his flute and mandolin, he fled, just as his stepmother was reaching the edge of the canal.

As he travelled, he met a man who went with him. He told him his story and his companion immediately started to reproach him for his treatment of the woman.

'What if she caught a fever? What if she drowned?'

But now the man argued, 'I did not choose to be ridden by her. I did what was necessary. What would you have done?'

Nevertheless, he still felt some self-reproach and promised this time that he would champion the cause of a dispossessed widow. But the judge, for it was he again, sent a message ahead to the queen.

In the west the land was green: green with moss, green with grass. The rivers were full of foaming green water and there, sun-bronzed men and women rode horses and fought with the dark-skinned wild people. He heard the drums the dark-skins played, so bartered for one and taught himself rhythm. Soon he found the dispossessed woman and, unsuspecting, started to read the papers that she showed him. As soon as his attention was engaged, she came behind him and with one bound was on his back. At once he was entranced again, but not so far that he could not feel resentment and his eyes moved to and fro, looking for escape. The queen, for it was she, hung on with one foot and one hand and cried, 'Now I have you! Now I have you! You must sleepwalk where I send you and carry me forever!'

He did this for one year, and then he remembered his friend the bird and threw himself and his burden in front of a galloping horse, so she had to loose him for fear of being trampled. Three whistles he gave, and at once the bird appeared. 'Go north, go north!'

'Yes!' he cried, as he shouldered his bag with his drum, mandolin, and flute and with a glance at his stepmother getting painfully to her feet, he strode off.

Once again he fell in with another, who reproached him yet again with his treatment of the queen, his stepmother.

'This sounds awfully familiar,' he said, looking at his companion quizzically. Yet he allowed himself to be persuaded to visit a woman who could give him good advice. Once again the judge sent word to the queen.

The north land was black: black beneath the dripping branches of the never-ending forest; black cliffs over seething grey seas; dark churches and chapels overshadowed by smoke and industry; black glistening pavements; even black snow where the soot had fallen. Men there argued, church and state and learning divided from each other and within themselves by the power of the word. Reason and reason and reason!

He learned eloquence and the art of speech, to such good effect that he was presented with a sword in honour of his learning. On his guard now, he presented himself at the house of the woman who could advise him. Yet, in one moment's loss of attention, she was on his back, hanging on by one hand. 'Now I have you! Now I have you! You must sleepwalk where I send you and carry me forever!'

For a whole day he carried her, then he heard the cry of the bird within. 'Sluggard, sluggard! Will you stay under your stepmother's spell forever?'

'No!' he cried and with great firmness removed his stepmother's hand from his throat. 'I am going home!' he declared and with a curt nod, left his stepmother, carrying his bag with his drum, his mandolin, and his flute, with his sword hanging at his side.

Once again he had a travelling companion. 'Are you going to rebuke me?' he asked.

'I? No. I have been too long in your stepmother's service. She has not treated me well, either. I sense my time has come. I can no longer pull the wool over your eyes. I will die soon. But let me give you one word of advice, and this time it comes from the heart. When you meet your stepmother again, cut off her head!'

The judge was sinking fast and the man stayed with him to comfort him until he had died. Then he buried him under the leaves, by a still lake. He planted the grove with tulip bulbs.

He approached the dark castle called Sleep. As he came near the gate opened and through it came his stepmother. 'My darling boy, my child; come to my arms; let me nurse you; let me rock you to sleep!'

'No, stepmother, that will not be. Your power over me is at an end. I have fought for wakefulness and now it is mine!'

Her face contorted in fury. 'Wakefulness, indeed! That's what you want! All right then, wake up, wake up, WAKE UP!'

'Not at your bidding, stepmother!' he said, and with one stroke severed her head from her shoulders.

There was a great swirling of dark mist. Slowly he awoke to find himself. The castle was still there, but transformed; glistening white stone, with the sun shining on turret and pinnacle and dancing on the waters of the moat. Everywhere there were banners and pennons, and over the covered drawbridge moved crowds of men and women and children, brightly clad. At the very centre of the castle was a golden dome, on which was seated the bird of wisdom. Over the gate were carved the sun and moon, and the name: the Castle of Night and Day.

Where his stepmother had stood was a woman, full of dignity, gravity, wisdom, and beauty, who, raising one arm towards the castle, said, 'Your inheritance'.

eight *Explaining Jim's story*

This is such an accomplished story it's difficult to believe that it is Jim's first piece of creative writing. We can see the technician in him at work in the structure, yet the unconscious flow moves compellingly throughout. Some people write autobiographically, but Jim chose the genre of fairy tale as his medium. The traditional fairy tale use of repetition mirrors the natural repetition of the process he describes. Until we become more aware of ourselves, we all fall into the trap of the same habitual patterns of behaviour many times. But as we begin to 'awaken', we find that it takes less time to catch ourselves and make a more conscious choice, retrieving the situation. Remember the poem *From the Source* in chapter three?

The setting

Let's look at how the story came to be, treating it as if it were a dream, which in part it is, and using some of the things we have covered in the book so far, starting with the setting. The story begins 'There was a dark castle called Sleep' and with those words, the scene is skilfully and symbolically set to describe Jim's childhood environment. A castle is usually a well-defended structure, situated in a commanding position with fortifications and far-reaching views. Not an easy place to get in or out of. And we learn that this is a 'dark' castle. One cannot see clearly in the dark; it is full of shadows and hidden things.

The castle is called Sleep, suggesting the condition that befalls all those who enter there. Sleep, in fairy tale, can indicate a state of unconsciousness, a loss of a sense of self, as in Sleeping Beauty's one hundred year sleep and occasionally a '…sleep unto death itself'. In this state, a healthy ego cannot develop and the sleeper cannot therefore make appropriate, or indeed any life choices, having no autonomy or energy. It is an unnatural, dreamless sleep, a kind of developmental limbo. Jim says he was under a spell, cast by the queen, in thrall to her, held in a sort of enchantment. The only one who seems to be awake, conscious of what she is about, is the queen. This gives her total control over all those who dwell within the castle's confines.

In this castle there is no king, which in such tales speaks of an absent father. Jim's parents divorced when he was young, at a time when divorce was much less common and acceptable than it is today. So this is the queen's domain, where she reigns supreme. Even out of the castle, her subjects would still be within her realm. They would need to travel far to escape her influence, as does our hero, for that is what Jim becomes in the telling. But as the story begins, he is just a small boy with so little sense of self that he does not once refer to himself as a prince, which is what the son of a queen must surely be. There are many tales of princes who have been dispossessed, denied their inheritance and do not know who they truly are. Quite often it is some Dark Feminine figure such as the Stepmother, with her inability or disinclination to adequately mother the child in her care, who brings this about.

Great demands and expectations are placed upon the children of kings and queens. They are set apart from other children and have to observe strict codes of behaviour. Such children can grow up with little contact with other children in the neighbourhood, as Jim did. They may grow to feel that they are different from other children, which can lead to difficulty in establishing peer relationships, and so they experience feelings of loneliness and isolation. This tendency often carries through into adult life.

The characters

The queen or stepmother is in fact Jim's infantile perception of his mother. He consciously chose to call her stepmother in the writing as a distancing device, enabling him to view her more clearly and gain some detachment as he wrote. This choice also came out of an understanding that this dark aspect of his mother is not the whole of her, and out of respect, as he did not want to betray her. Perhaps there was still some vestigial sense of the child's loyalty or guilt, inspired by the judge. Yet we all know how stepmothers are in fairy tales! She is also a queen, which indicates the power and authority this figure holds for Jim, both as child and young man.

With benefit of adult hindsight, Jim could see that his mother had a hidden affectionate and caring side. He intuited that she was terrified of her sexuality. But as a child he experienced her as emotionally cold, detached, unrelational, self-contained, and undemonstrative. She was at the same time demanding, needy, and possessive of her son.

A woman behaving in this manner may be seen as being possessed by her inner Masculine or animus, hiding behind whom there is usually a frightened inner child. This type of animus, originally developed to defend the mother when she was a child, constructs the fortress of protection that eventually becomes a prison: in this case, the castle. Effectively the child of an animus-dominated woman has no mother. Her feminine, nurturing, relational nature has never been allowed to develop. It has been sacrificed to the jealously possessive animus, causing the inner Feminine to remain undifferentiated and in a regressive childlike state. It is this unconscious and needy child, masquerading as the queen, who truly binds Jim to her, holding him in the bonds of her own fear.

She was obviously a heavily judgemental woman, aided as she is by the judge, who fills Jim with feelings of guilt should he ever think of disappointing or abandoning her. If we live with judgement, we learn to judge and inevitably Jim took in his mother's way of being to some extent, developing an inner judge of his own. This is the figure that accompanies him each time he tries to escape with his blandishments of loyalty and duty. This judge is also a bit of a Trickster, a secret agent for the queen, fooling the boy easily at first.

The queen, then, unconsciously inflicts her own restrictive pattern on her children, conditioning them to live within her own limited parameters, the fairy tale castle. So we see that the queen is symbolically imprisoned too, in this dark and deadening place.

Perhaps the unrecognized frightened inner child in Jim's mother felt that he was all that she had left to hold on to since the divorce, and so clung tightly to him, dreading being alone. She is clearly the dominant character in the story, appearing in many guises throughout.

As dreamwork progressed and, bit by bit, Jim began to piece together his story through dreams, he shared with us many remembered vignettes of how life was for him as a child. The reasonable adult part of him was always quick to come in with the redeeming comment, recognizing how difficult life must have been for his mother too, as a divorced woman having to cope alone. But the feeling tone of the relationship, as opposed to the rational explanation, is strikingly portrayed in the following dreams, which contributed considerably to his story.

'I am lying in a bed, face down. A woman is lying on top of me. She seems to have arms and legs all over the place, and struggle as I might, I cannot get out. I can't see her – she might be invisible! I feel desperate. I recite the Lord's Prayer at her, with no effect. In fact, she joins in. Then I say, "In God's name go," with all the power I can manage, and I wake up.'

Here in this dream is the gift of the motif central to Jim's story, which helps us to understand something of how the story came to be. It gives a graphic metaphor for the intuitively perceived mother and child relationship, which was then carried forward disastrously into future relationships with women. Jim knew that the figure on his back was that of his mother because of the two earlier dreams, which follow.

'I am in a bedroom with my mother, in twin beds, with a bedside cabinet between us. I have woken with a start and called, "Mum, mummy, mum!" remembering that previously she had not come. And now I hear her get out of bed and run towards me, in her nightdress. But she runs and runs and never gets nearer, but I don't want her to. I cry, "Go away!" in terror, but can't make myself heard. I can't move. I wake up abruptly.'

Now we begin to find the darkness in the story. It is simply the mother's presence that evokes such terror. The child's longing for the reassurance of good mothering causes him to call out for her, but even as he calls he remembers that previously she hadn't come.

So there would seem to be a history of the good enough mother not being there when Jim needed her. Only the Dark Mother heeds his call.

Getting in touch with his feelings again through this dream caused Jim to remember a nightmare he had had twenty years ago, which still gives him goosebumps as he recounts it today. He cannot remember any other dream having so powerful an effect on him, and says that it was highly realistic.

The waking circumstances at the time of this dream were that Jim was visiting his mother in the family home. There was some sort of domestic upheaval, decorating perhaps, which resulted in everyone sleeping in different places. Jim slept in the bed that his mother usually slept in.

'I was in that same bed. The door opened and my mother came in and looked down at me. I woke totally, instantly, and found myself sitting bolt upright and screaming!'

Only when it is imperative that we become aware of something that seriously threatens our wellbeing are we sent a nightmare like this. It is a way of getting our attention by showing us the force of feeling that is being repressed.

Dreams such as this are also trying to awaken us to the fact that some frightening dynamic from the past is once again at work in our lives. That the perceived threat is still as real now as it ever was. For although this dream came when Jim was in his mid-thirties, in essence it is a child's dream. So we might say that Jim's inner child sub-personality is the one having this nightmare, since the adult would hardly be likely to respond to the mother so. Certainly it made its mark, in that Jim can easily remember it, with the associated feeling of terror still present some twenty years on.

Yet the mother doesn't do anything; she just looks down at him! It is not uncommon when a mother and her boy child live alone for her to treat him as the man of the house, expecting more of him than any child can give. Sometimes this expectation is unconsciously carried into the realm of sexuality too. The mother may not be aware of it, and may never overtly attempt any kind of abusive behaviour, yet the sensitive child may pick up on something uncomfortably disturbing in his mother's possessive attitude. Not understanding what is going on, he becomes afraid and wary of her.

All of these dreams share the bedroom, with the boy in bed as their setting. So we naturally wonder if there was something of this nature that was part of the darkness in the castle. Did the stepmother cross some boundary of intimacy in some way with her child? Jim has no memories of anything sexual taking place between them, and I would not really expect that it did, but certainly something frightened him. Perhaps he sensed an unconscious unrealized desire in her and felt disempowered by the queen's very powerful, controlling personality that could so easily overwhelm him in other respects.

Though disturbed by this frightening dream when it occurred, Jim, like most of us, would not have known what to do with it. His astute Dream Maker, knowing that Jim was now on a dreamwork course and at last paying serious attention to the messages in his dreams, seized upon the chance to lead Jim back to his childhood experience. More than that, the dreams show that the inner child is still suffering from the terror connected with his mother's presence, just as he did all those years ago.

When this happens it is usually because the sensitive child's antennae has sensed something similarly threatening developing right now. This stirs up the old fears, and enduring the repeat experience in the present leaves the child hopeless, feeling that nothing has changed. He feels he is still a virtual prisoner in the castle, at the mercy of the stepmother queen.

When Jim came into dreamwork he had been unhappily married and divorced and then in a long-term relationship that had recently ended. At the time these dreams took place he was feeling trapped in his failing marriage. His difficult relationship with his wife was recreating the effect of his life in the castle that had affected him so deeply as a child. His wife had, in his inner child's eyes at least, assumed the mantle of the queen. When there are unresolved feelings around our relationship with our parents we tend to find partners who carry the same attitudes and qualities as a parent, or have the latent potential to develop this kind of behaviour.

The symbols
The bird
In Jim's story, the bird that calls at his window and disturbs his deathly sleep also breaks the spell. It is a kind of messenger, mediating the prompting from the part of Jim that is eager to heal. It comes to awaken the young man to himself and to start him upon the quest he needs to make to free himself from his mother's clutches. It is winged, as was Hermes or Mercury, messenger of the gods in ancient Greek mythology. Birds are often associated with spirit or the higher Self. Seeing one in a context such as this can cause us to lift our gaze and attention to a different perspective, encouraging us to take a bird's eye view of a situation.

Jim describes this bird as almost like a pelican. It is a big gawky bird, at home in the air and in water; something that can bridge these elements, which are often seen as representing the mind and feelings respectively. Without doubt, during the course of his dreamwork, Jim's engineer's mind swooped and soared many times when he connected with his symbols and feelings and sought to understand them.

The feather that the bird leaves behind is a kind of talisman, a reminder of the message, to keep it alive in Jim's consciousness once the bird itself has flown. These intuitions are fleeting when they appear and often we miss or mistrust them, or forget. The message said, 'Go east' and marked the start of Jim's journey of homecoming into selfhood and the claiming of his inheritance.

The four directions
• The east is commonly associated with the dawn, hope, and youth – a great place for the boy to begin his necessary journey of separation from mother.
• The south, which he visited next, is connected with the noonday sun, fire, warmth, and the solar, Masculine principle. It is a good choice for the next phase as the boy begins to grow up.

• The west has the sunset, autumn, is associated with middle age and can be seen as the place of death. Maybe it is the 'little death' of the enslaved boy?

• The north is a place of cold and darkness. It symbolizes old age and is known as the land of the dead. Again we meet the theme of death. As the hero grows stronger he can support the frightened child, and the judge carries less energy and influence.

As he made his circular journey the boy met all sorts of people who taught him new skills. He learnt melody, harmony, rhythm – new skills for a boy who has lived in cold isolation. They all depend on good relationship with the other musicians who take part in the process of making music together.

But in each place he stopped he also met another woman who turned out to be his mother in disguise. His marriage and his other significant relationships were all doomed because they arose out of his misplaced loyalty to his mother, of which the judge always reminded him. There must have been great guilt around any new loving relationship, which would on some level have felt like implicit betrayal of the queen.

The sword

In his final stopping place, the boy learns the art of speech. Now at last he can speak his own mind, his truth. He is rewarded with a sword, symbol of power, protection, and the Masculine principle again, traditionally wielded by the archetypal Hero. The sword can also be seen as the active aspect of the will and has supernatural powers – remember Excalibur, the 'sword in the stone' claimed by the British King Arthur?

The symbol of the sword tells us that the boy has grown into the man and can at last be free. Not just of his mother, but of the judge too. For once the man becomes able to discriminate fairly for himself, the judge begins to fade away. I remember Jim doing a most dignified and moving piece of visualization around the death of the judge. This exercise, along with revisiting the dream, hadn't always been easy for him, but this time there was such depth and quiet authority evident as Jim respectfully laid the judge to rest. He expressed his gratitude for the way he had protected him when he was a frightened child and assured him that he had now found a better way and was strong enough to look after the inner child himself. I find that dreamworkers instinctively know what ritual or ceremony is needed, creating it spontaneously for themselves as they reach an ending or new beginning and honour the Death and Rebirth archetype.

With this behind him, Jim was able to deal with his stepmother, the queen. Since animus-driven women tend to live in their heads much of the time, it is entirely appropriate that he cuts of her head with his sword. There are times when we have to have the courage to use the sword, to be merciless when there is no other way. Only then, when the queen is dead, can come the magical moment of transformation.

In all the best fairy tales, this is really more connected with restoration. The little boy was always a prince. The wonderful inheritance, though denied him, was in truth always his. And see how the castle changes now!

The transformation

The darkness has gone, the sun shines, there is a golden dome, signifying the solar, Masculine, spiritual principles, crowned by the bird of wisdom. A person entering would see the carving of the sun and moon, suggesting balance and harmony between the archetypal Masculine and Feminine principle, where there had been such imbalance before.

Finally there is the woman full of dignity, gravity, wisdom, and beauty. She could be the exact opposite of the cold, dark stepmother. We have to recognize though, strange as it seems, that both of these feminine figures will be part of Jim's anima, his woman within. Jim recognized that he had taken on some of his mother's dark characteristics, and this recognition allowed him to move on. Now he can stand as man, archetypal Hero, and prince, to look upon the positive face of the Feminine, the loving woman who hands over to him the inheritance he has worked so hard to redeem.

Happily, just around the time the course ended, Jim met and fell in love with a woman who broke the mould. She was quite unlike anyone he had formed an intimate relationship with before, and carried many of the qualities of this new dream figure. They later married and are still truly and contentedly devoted to each other, several years later, and are still happy.

I hope that Jim's story and my explanation of the dynamics at work in it have helped to show you what is possible if you stay with dreamwork. The story that follows is very different, and speaks of one woman's road of trials, from which she emerges as a person of immense courage and caring.

nine *Helen's story*

The Rose and the Key

Once upon a time a little girl was born to a king and queen who lived in the south of England, near the sea. They already had one son and the queen was hoping for a daughter, so she was delighted when the child was born, even though she had not planned to have another so soon.

The little princess was late arriving, so late that when she was born she was blue and cold. The midwife wrapped her in a blanket and put her in a cot, telling the queen that she would warm up. After the first night she was cuddled and fed and kept warm by her mother, who hoped that the little girl would become a great and powerful queen one day and would perhaps break the curse that hung over the family. So they named her Helen after a great and tragic queen. Unfortunately the older brother was very jealous of the new baby daughter and so, when she was only six weeks old, the queen stopped holding her close and feeding her. Instead she propped her up in her cradle with a bottle, and left her to feed herself.

The curse that haunted the family was made manifest in a number of ways. One of the things it did was subject the king and queen to a great thirst that made them hunger after a potion that would make them fade, so that you could hardly see them any more. The potion had more of a hold over the king than the queen. When he drank it, it made him feel strong and gave him a belief in himself that at other times he failed to have. He would leave the castle to go and drink and laugh and joke with other men as big and strong as he was. These kings of their castles would gather daily to compete and barter and steal from each other, to stick out their chests and view their domains, secretly counting their gold and drowning their dreams together in the bottom of their glasses of lies.

Sometimes the king and queen would drink together and sometimes only the king would drink. Either way, when the potion was drunk it would make them become cloudy and half disappear into a mist, so that the children could no longer find them. The king and queen would become so lost and frightened that they would fight with each other to try to find their way out of the mist. The king would look to the queen to save him from the ghosts and ghouls that haunted him in the mist. The queen looked to the king to save her from these ghosts, but neither could, so they ended up hating each other. After a while they looked to their children to save them, whispering and pleading under their breath, but the children did not know how. They also became lost in the mist that surrounded the whole house so that it became cut off from the outside world. During this time, the little ones would creep about waiting, as they knew that the house would stay like this until the pleading and anger ended.

The king considered the women of his household – his wife and daughter – to be slaves, there either to please or serve him. After he had been out drinking with the other big strong men, he would become silent, moody, and deeply withdrawn. Sometimes he returned home in a rage and would beat the queen late at night. Then the little princess would be unable to sleep, hearing her mother's screams.

At these times the queen would long to break free from her prison, to be free of their castle, in which she was kept. Every day she would lay the table with wonderful food for the little ones, watching them grow big and strong, healthy and rosy cheeked. Yet she herself would refuse to eat, or secretly regurgitate the food later in the bathroom. Maybe she hoped that she would one day be able to slip through the cracks in the door and make her escape on a ship bound for Africa, where she would be recognized as a queen. But she was never able to get quite thin enough.

The king became more and more silent as the years passed. He watched his little girl, but never spoke to her. He watched her grow, and loved the way she looked. Both he and the queen would look into Helen's eyes and see that she also had been born with the family curse. This made them sad. The king turned away from them even more. The queen instructed Helen on how to be a good, well-mannered girl who would love everybody and be loved back. She also instructed her family never to mention the family curse.

Every so often the old, wizened, wise Grandmothers would visit, and secretly pray for the family. Helen knew that they were praying, but also that they felt too old and feeble to help. She watched as they took out their eyes when they came to the door, knowing that they could not bear what they saw. One was tall and frail and weak-hearted. She always smelled beautiful and Helen knew that she was really an angel that had fallen to earth as a young woman and was waiting patiently to be taken back. She kept a rose for Helen, but died too soon to be able to tell her where it was.

The other was small and walnut-coloured. She had come from the fairy folk, the dwellers under the hill. She clacked her knitting needles and smoked tobacco continuously, telling the children of the pain of life and the great pain in their family history. She had yellow fingers and a husky voice. She held the secrets of the fairies. This grandmother had a key that she kept for Helen, but she also died too soon to tell her where the key was.

The mist had enveloped the house for longer than Helen could remember. Sometimes it seemed to her that she was living in a deep dark place, not a castle at all. The king would tell her that the queen was on the brink of madness and that Helen must help her and be strong for her. Her mother would whisper to Helen that it was her father who was trying to drive her mad, and that sometimes she feared for her sanity. Helen lived in a world where mind spells were played constantly. She found them everywhere. She searched for the clues in the words and feelings and became very good at understanding what they really meant.

After many years of this, the king and queen were so unhappy they felt they could no longer live with each other's sorrow. They separated and the king went to live in a large crumbling castle with many towers, by the sea, whilst the children stayed with the queen. The king married again, and, from then on, Helen rarely saw him. His new wife had two children of her own and wanted them to inherit the king's riches. So she locked the doors and kept the king's old family at a distance. The wife was very clever but also afraid of the power the children might have over the king. She would therefore make spells to cloud his vision even more, promising him comfort and warmth, safety in her arms. She banished all who came near him, even his fairy mother, who was brought to the house old, crippled, and dying. The castle they lived in had its own potion palace, so the king could now spend his days swilling golden liquid and drowning his guilt.

Both Helen's grandmothers died and no one spoke of them any more. To Helen, they became distant memories. Her mother, wishing to keep her away from the pain of death, kept her away from the funerals. To Helen it seemed that there was no space for death or real grief; it remained hidden underground. It was kept with the key and the rose in a deep dark place surrounded by a mist, always close, though Helen could never quite discover exactly where.

When Helen became a woman, her mother no longer wanted her in the house. The queen took in many lovers with her charms and wanted no competition. Watching her, Helen learned about the power of sexual desire. She understood the control that it held.

Helen was eager to leave, but since there was no prince to take her hand, she had to journey alone, not really knowing where she would go or how it would be. However, she also feared that she would have to spend some of her life in mourning. She tried to put this out of her mind when she opened the door and smelled the crisp, clear air that beckoned her away from the family home. As Helen was leaving, the queen gave her a purple dress and dancing shoes, and she put them on.

Helen had many adventures when she left home. She found the powerful magnetism of her own sexual desire. She danced and laughed and loved with many people. She found out that there were many people to love in the big wide world, but if she stayed too long they could pull her down into confusion and complication and she would begin to touch that deep dark place that she wanted to escape from. It seemed so small, that place, something that she could fit into the palm of her hand. But the power of it, if it were released, could destroy her, and she knew that there were people out there who might release it if she allowed them to come too close for too long.

So she would love them and kiss them and look deeply into their eyes. She let them look into her and share her bed. She kept snakes and doves and jewels under her dress, around her ankles, and in her hair, and she would let her lovers touch and taste these precious things. The queen had taught her well. In her encounters, she and her lovers would open up each other's depth and passion, but, fearing that love would overwhelm her and leave her out of control, she would tie up her lovers with silken threads of promises and paint rainbows on their chests. She would leave them with their broken hearts and bewilderment, and take her purple dress and dancing shoes and dance on. People got hurt. Men were blamed for everything that was bad in the world. Were they being sacrificed because of her father's betrayal?

For a while, Helen worked with children who did not know she was a princess, listening to them, helping them, and learning how to play. She had a dog as her companion and she danced around her own country, then further afield, across the water, living in magical places, wild places, by oceans; on mountains, in crazy, arty cities. She learned the language of the stars, a magnificent ancient language that opened up her mind and her heart. She accumulated books of planetary wisdom and learned to draw up charts. Then she began to understand the ticking of hearts and minds and souls.

Gradually her role changed. She realized one day that a baby was growing in her womb and that soon she would become a mother. The father of the child, a man who excited her and scared her, moved in with her, and they made a home together. Through the birth of her first daughter came a transformation! Helen was surprised by the natural way she took to this role, to rocking and feeding, carrying, and knowing what her baby needed. She felt that she already knew this child well, that they had known each other for more than a thousand years.

There was an intensity of passionate love between them that Helen never remembered experiencing before, a bliss and an awareness that she could never have imagined. After the birth she lay with her baby all night and the next day, basking in the beauty that had emerged from her body. But then the physician came and told her that her baby was very sick and must be taken to a wise old doctor who might be able to heal her. Her baby was taken away from her and she was left with her pain, her bewilderment, and her prayers. The baby's father stayed with the little girl's suffering body while the doctors gave her new blood and then put her into a clean, warm, dry, and airy place to try to get the yellow out of her. Later, when Helen came home from hospital, she felt stripped, violated, and shocked.

Though the years with the man eventually brought another daughter, their relationship was messy and complicated, bringing many tears and much anger and hurt. His pain and anger were too great for Helen. Maybe it touched her own pain so distressingly that she could not bear it. Finally, she banished him from her home and her life.

By this time, she was back in her own country. The old king, her father, had become very ill and could no longer move or speak. Helen had a home, two children, and her memories. She had, though, neglected to honour the power of the piece of darkness that had stayed with her since childhood. Her purple dress and dancing shoes had been lost. The jewels were trampled in the dust, the snakes slithered into darkness, and the doves had flown to the treetops.

Because of her neglect, out of the darkness crept a spell that changed her into a frightened, fearful rabbit. Her home became a dark and dusty warren, a twilight place, although within it she loved her daughters well enough. She hugged and fed and clothed them, yet crawled away from the light, allowing only other women near. She needed to rest. There were bleak days when she felt that only the rabbit hole was safe. She felt that she had lost so much and was so painfully close to the dark place.

More and more she stayed at home, frightened that her furry body might be seen and condemned. She realized that if people looked too closely into her eyes they would see a frightened rabbit living there, and that maybe they would take her only loves, her only meaning, away from her. She kept quieter, and more silent. She retreated deeper into her hole. Occasionally she would look into her star books, but the bleakness stopped her from gaining any wisdom or comfort for herself or others.

After a long time, though, she could hide it no longer. Her fears and paranoia were keeping her from sleeping. They were making her heart beat faster, so that she thought that she might be near to death. Someone told her about a woman who might listen to her, who might hold a key. She decided to go and see her. The woman listened, then held out a key so that Helen could take it, and the spell was broken! She was no longer a rabbit but a woman again. It took her a long while to pull off the fur and the tail and the long ears, and it was painful. The fur had penetrated deeply and had torn at her skin, leaving scars and red welts that took a while to heal, but she knew she was healing. For some time Helen had to go about naked – with no purple dress or shoes. She longed for them, mourned for them, and dreamed of them.

Many new people came into her life over the next few years. She began to open up her heart again to people other than her children. She felt taller and lighter. Her key was opening many doors, both dark and light. She learned to accept the chaos of life. She never knew if the door she was opening held pain or joy, but she knew that she was opening doors to life and to the possibility of love.

Helen dug out the warren that they had been living in and made windows to allow in the light. She painted it so that she could see the dark corners. The snakes slithered back. She built a dovecote and swept up the dust to find her jewels. Her children planted roses in the garden, but still she was naked and very cold in the winter.

One day she found among the roses a star that had fallen from the sky and had been pierced by the thorns of one of the roses in the garden. She picked it up and, as she felt it, she realized that the same star had been in her dreams and it had come to tell her something. It had fallen from the sky, where dreams are composed, and where the stars that she studied were living. It was woven from golden threads of dreams that she had known and would know, that held her secrets, her hopes, her desires, and her fears. She sensed that the star would lead her to a guide, and so she waited.

Someone who saw her holding the star one day told her of a woman who could help her unravel the threads of her life and weave dream stars. Helen realized then that this was her path, to weave dream stars for herself and for others. She found the woman and opened herself to learn from her. The dreaming woman handed back Helen's purple dress and shoes. They had been embroidered on, so were even more beautiful than ever before, and fitted perfectly. They had been kept safely until she could wear them again. Helen began to dance, and to pass on her knowledge of the stars to others.

With the dreaming woman, Helen discovered more wounds that she carried and the bruises that rough hands had made when she was still a child. She learnt how to make a salve from the roses in her garden that would soothe her wounds and bruises. More stars fell from the sky and were pierced by the thorns in her rose garden. Helen freed them gently and kept them in a box by her bed until they healed and she could re-weave them together. When she was disentangling them from the brambles, she was often frightened by the little ghosts and spooks that had found their homes in the roots of the rose bushes. As she shook the stars free, they would often shriek and wail, and frighten her, as they used to frighten her in the mists of childhood with their loud voices and shrill high wails. Yet, as she shook the bushes, they would scuttle away, out of her garden, their little arms and legs and naked spindly bodies melting away as the sunlight shone on them. Helen planted more flowers in between the roses. She knew they would take a while to grow, but she felt that the roses' thorns would protect these more delicate wild flowers, which would add more colour to her garden.

Now Helen is with her Prince. He came from far away to find her as she called for him in her dreams at night. She left her voice and strands of hair in the forest where he lived, to guide him to her side. He came with a magic sword and golden shield to protect her. He had fought many monsters in his time and carried on his belt a magic potion that reminded her of her childhood.

He brought his own ghosts, and one of them would sit on his shoulder and torment him from time to time to drink his potion.

And from time to time he would succumb. He would drink and fill the house with unconsciousness, with mists and spooks and whispers and wails. Helen would be drawn in, as if drowning, and lose herself again. She would wrap herself in a black cloak and rub mud in her hair. The ghost that sits on his shoulder can also jump onto hers and mix up her thoughts and fears. Just when she thinks that she exists no more, her bright lover returns and holds her and trusts her and loves her so sweetly that she forgets the madness – until the next time.

She knows now that the spell has not yet been broken. Although she has the roses and the key, she still needs to learn to use them better. Maybe she will need to pass them on to her children when the time comes.

Helen is now carrying her third child, who seems to hold in its uncertain heart either greater joys or the biggest heartbreak a woman must ever experience. She knows that we have no control, our destiny is what it is. Her future is uncertain and she is scared. All she can try to do is keep herself open, knowing that her baby needs her love, however long or short its life may be. She needs to be prepared as she goes into the madness in her heart and soul, the madness of grief, from which she knows some never return.

All Helen can do is to remember to hold onto others, to stay close and to look in the right places for those who can guide and support her. Although she is on her own, she knows she also shares her grief with others, some of whom she knows, and others that she has never seen – for grief is universal.

Sometimes she is overwhelmed by the millions of broken hearts and the amount of grief that one small heart can bear. She wants to look into every bereaved mother's eyes and hold the dead babies that haunt their souls. She sends a prayer to the unborn child who shares her body, touches her soul, and tests her faith.

ten 10 *Explaining Helen's story*

At the time of writing her story, Helen also wrote a prayer which took the form of a letter to her unborn child. She shared this prayer with her dream group at the end of her storytelling. This was deeply moving, an intense emotional experience that brought an already supportive group even closer. Helen's baby had been diagnosed with a heart problem while still in the womb and we were all aware of her anxiety as her pregnancy progressed. She shared the following dream which she had when she was first expecting her baby:

Cracked egg dream

'I am looking at a cupboard. It is wooden. The door is open. It contains hundreds of brown eggs on shelves. There is a warm glow to the light...I look down into a basket that I have. It is a wicker basket. There are three eggs in my basket. One is damaged, as though it has been dropped and so has a small circular crack on it. There is a feeling of acceptance.'

She continues: 'I had this dream when pregnant with my son, in the early days when we were not sure how bad his heart condition would be. The crack in the egg was round like a heart, more like a little smash than a long crack.'

This dream speaks for itself, and seemed to presage what was to come. When Helen's baby boy was born, the parents were told that he would need complicated heart surgery in infancy if he were to survive. The decision to operate was delayed repeatedly to give the baby a chance to grow stronger. By the time he was two years old, the doctors thought he was as strong and well as he would ever be, and the date was fixed.

Tragically the little boy died during the operation, a terrible shock for his parents who had taken him into hospital a happy, healthy, lively child and now had to return home without him. The loss of a child is terrible, and our hearts went out to Helen and her family.

Along with most of Helen's dream group, I attended the baby's funeral; all of us steeling ourselves to face the pain of the sad, ceremonial farewell and the effect that it would have on our friend. Helen was awesome. She'd planned a beautiful ceremony that gently honoured her baby's life and death.

Helen stood to speak, asking us to remember the happy child alongside the tragic one. She recounted tales of her little boy's escapades and we found ourselves sharing moments of spontaneous laughter in among our tears. Helen behaved with dignity, composure, and compassion, showing a nobility of spirit that inspired us all. Here truly stood the great queen.

There is no fairy tale ending to this story, but rather a mythic cycle of prediction and omens, fate and tragedy. We have to remember that this is also a modern story and that unlike the fairy tale, life does go on and may well not be 'happy ever after'. Yet at the very darkest moment Helen's radiant spirit shone through and we could see that she would, indeed, go on.

Understanding the story

To understand more of this particular story and to help you to see how it all came together for Helen, I'd like to take you back to the beginning now. To the little princess who spent the first night of her life separated from her mother. Such children can experience overwhelming feelings of isolation and abandonment when the rightful bonding with the mother cannot take place. For some, the bond is never formed, and there may then be a lack of closeness in their relationship. Some choose subconsciously to remain distanced from a close relationship with anyone, always at the edge of things, slow to trust or join in. Helen's separation from her mother was taken a step further because of sibling rivalry, which her mother clearly did not handle well at the time. So the little girl's natural need for maternal love, touch, and affection was not fulfilled.

Helen's name

There is already an emerging theme of emotional distancing, alienation, and isolation by the time the parents choose to name Helen. The naming of a child is a most significant act, giving word to the image the parent carries, and their expectation of how the child will be. Such an expectation can sit heavily upon a child, even if it is never spoken. The child's early connection with the mother is so finely attuned that it is believed that the infant can 'sense into' the mother's unconscious imagery, receiving the message symbiotically, even as the intent is formed in the mother's mind.

In a way Helen's destiny was spelled out when she was christened Helen, and the name made clear her task. She was to become great and powerful so that she might break the family curse; something her mother could not do. Yet her namesake, Helen of Troy, was flawed as well as tragic. Was there a darker expectation here? Would power carry a price tag? Would something have to be sacrificed to greatness sooner or later? There's an intimation of a kind of mythic doom here. The name itself almost becomes a curse, Helen's own curse to carry, the responsibility for breaking the family curse that may well have afflicted generations.

The potion and the curse

Alcoholism is a curse that has destroyed families the world over for longer than we can remember. The children in these families have to try to base their lives on shifting sands. Behaviour that is praised when the parent is sober may be reviled when they are drunk. The child does not know how best to behave in order to stay safe and relatively unscathed. Their instincts are continually denied, there is no constancy of experience to learn from, and they may well go on to have great difficulty in making decisions or adjusting to unexpected changes, having experienced all such change as threatening. Living with inconsistent boundaries, these children find it extremely difficult to trust themselves, let alone others.

They also experience painful and frightening feelings of abandonment when the parents 'fade' and are lost to them in the hazy mists of their addiction. They become orphans, time and time again, hostages to the irresponsible drunken whim of the 'shade' of the father or mother who was there before. Here are the beginnings of Helen's ghosts – insubstantial, without conscience or accountability, haunting child and parent alike.

These ghosts bring guilt and shame that no one must see, leading into another demand of the curse: secrecy. We are told that the queen instructs her children in this art. When we collude in keeping someone else's dark guilty secret, we cannot help taking some of their guilt and shame onto ourselves. It spreads its stealthy contamination through the family in a tissue of deceit and denial that supports the addiction and betrays the young child's instinct for truth.

The need for secrecy leads to isolation. Few children want to invite others back to play when the house may only be full of 'ghosts' after school, the parents lost again in their mists – and the parents in alcoholic families continually discourage visitors. Little to counteract the addiction finds its way in from outside and the children are unable to speak their truth, so this becomes a self-perpetuating reinforced pattern. The dark secret remains well disguised and within it the children endure a terror and confusion of which no one is aware.

In reading Helen's story, I was struck by the way she is able to write about such painful childhood memories without saying a word of how she felt as a child. We know something of how the mother feels, of her self-loathing and despair, but if you were to do the 'colouring your functions' exercise from chapter three with this story, you would find very little colour denoting feeling.

Helen conveys a strong sense of how it was to live in that situation without ever explicitly describing her emotions. When I mentioned this to her, we agreed that this goes to show how deeply ingrained the powerful early messages become. We may come to recognize them, but that is not the same as being able to overcome them, which can take a lifetime, perhaps many lifetimes, to achieve.

The grandmothers
Here, the grandmothers are the only visitors we know of, and as they are afflicted with the family curse themselves, they have to take their

eyes out as they enter the house, so terrible is the threat of what they might see. Yet what wonderful characters they are! There is a kind of balance between them, between the angelic spirit and the fairy-fey earth spirit, the sweet perfume of the rose and the pungent tobacco smoke, the one who is waiting to return to heaven and the other who is so securely connected to the earth.

The grandmothers often carry the fairy godmother role in fairy tales. They come bearing gifts, in this case the rose and the key, but, and here is the tragedy again, they die before they can give them to Helen. How often do we fail to say what we need to say to those close to us, holding back our gifts of wisdom and guidance, fearing to intrude? How often do we withdraw, our tongue tied by embarrassment, rather than reveal our deepest feelings? Life is short and it is not a rehearsal. None of us know when we will die. Speak out now, if you can. Don't leave it until it is too late.

The symbols

The rose

The gifts that these grandmothers bring are the rose and the key. Helen's maternal grandmother always smelled of roses, her favourite perfume. This is how Helen came to recognize the rose as her symbol. Helen also had several dreams of her own younger daughter, whom she had named Rose after her rosy grandmother. These dreams came when the little girl was three years old, an optimum time for a spurt of ego development when the child begins to sort out where she begins and her parents end. In repeatedly drawing Helen's attention to this time in Rose's life, her dreams were drawing her ever closer to the little 'rose child' within.

The rose has universal associations with romantic love, the heart, the French troubadour tradition, and a certain tenderness and sincerity of feeling. For Helen, though, the personal association is with her grandmother. Later in the story, she learned to plant and grow her own roses, as did her children. This shows that, in time and through hard work, she found for herself the truth her grandmother could not tell her, and passed it on to her daughters.

The key

The key has a much more explicit function. It both locks and unlocks – a hopeful sign for Helen. I was struck by the fact that this grandmother could speak of both her own and the family pain. Is this part of the significance of the symbol? Is this the 'key' to the way out, unlocking the prison of the family curse by telling of the secrets? It may be the key to the process of individuation, coming as it does at puberty, a time of ego development, and the transition from child to woman. Helen's dreams also offered her the symbol of a key:

The man in the shop

'I am a man running a shop. I am also me. We are on holiday. My husband can see a castle if he looks from a certain point. I'm sure I have been there before, but it's a vague memory.

'There is a murderer in the shop. Eventually he is killed somehow. The man is writing a manuscript about what happened and he thinks that it is likely that the murderer will even be able to get to the manuscript before it is published, even though he is now dead. Sure enough, the pages catch fire. He manages to beat the flames out so that only two have been destroyed. Always there is a threat of his being killed.

'He gets the manuscript and leaves the shop, closing the front door, but then he has to go back in to get the keys. It is dark; he has turned off the lights. It is really spooky. I am sure something horrible is going to get him, but no, he gets the keys and leaves the shop. He locks up. He uses the wrong key at first, then uses a long key, brassy, pointed, and ridged. It looks familiar.'

Helen said of this dream, 'It seems to be describing how it felt to unlock the feelings and the fears. Even though the physical danger is no longer there, the murderer's ghostly presence is felt. I had this dream long before I was aware that one day I would write my story, yet there the man is writing his experience of what happened. I had always been terrified of my father until he had a stroke when I was in my late twenties. Could he be the murderer in the dream? The key that looks familiar is similar to one my father used at the pub that he once owned. It is also similar to one my husband used, to unlock a place at work.'

The man in the shop in Helen's dream is also Helen. He has the key and can lock up and leave a dangerous situation, even if he takes time to find the right key. This is hopeful, but did you notice that the key in the dream relates both to Helen's father and her husband, and the pub, the 'potion palace' of Helen's childhood story? We'll take another look at these two key men in Helen's life later in this section, and we'll also see the key again, in connection with the symbol of the frightened rabbit.

The purple dress and shoes

The purple dress and shoes were suggested to Helen by many dreams of trying on clothes and shoes, trying to find an image that felt right for her. This is what many girls do in their teenage years, experimenting with different looks until something just clicks and feels absolutely right. Helen remembers this happening when she tried on a deep purple dress that really suited her. She felt empowered when wearing it, which is just what she needed when she left home to make her way in the world.

The colour purple has varied associated meanings, but for Helen I feel it held something unconventional, which allowed her to dance freely into an exciting new phase of her life. It is the colour used by bishops, carrying spirituality and dignity; the colour of royalty too, often used in ceremony.

The snake

The queen had also passed on another gift, the more double-edged art of seduction, which was to serve Helen well. Her writing is wonderfully seductive at times, bringing in the spellbinding symbolism of the snakes, doves and jewels, silken threads, and rainbows! What man wouldn't be tempted? It is the snake that hints at something darker. There are many tales of fairy women, half human, half serpent, who set aside one day of the week, usually a Saturday, when they hide themselves away, taking on their serpent form. The Sibyl was one, an oracle of Greek myth who lived in a cave. Then there was the winged Mesuline, from the French fairy tale tradition, who turned into a serpentine monster when out of her lover's sight.

We usually find watery images around this figure. She takes a bath, or swims in the lake in her serpent form. The singing sirens on the rocks of their island, who lure sailors to certain death, belong here. The mermaid and the selkie seal are part of this myth. Stories tell of seals becoming partly human when they fall in love with a mortal man. They try to follow his wishes and live with him on the land, but sooner or later they have to return to the water, to their serpent selves if they are to survive. Woe betide the hapless lover who catches a glimpse of her at this time! The relationship will be terminated in an instant, and she may even cast him into the lake to drown.

It's easy to see how this ties in with not letting the lovers get too close for too long, isn't it? When people's fundamental needs to be unconditionally loved and held, to belong, have been denied in childhood, they can end up caught between a longing for intimacy and a great fear of the vulnerability which is necessary to achieve such closeness. These sirens, the great seductresses of myth and legend, have an archetypal quality, not being fully human. The longing may cause them to develop great seductive skills, to draw men into intimate relationship. Yet the knowledge that she is different means the siren needs to keep one day out of seven to honour her serpent nature, so that she does not live in denial of this important part of herself, an archetypally dangerous thing to do.

And here is the 'secret' again! For the serpent has long been seen as a symbol of sexuality and the old feminine powers which the Christian patriarchs have been eager to sanitize and repress. When Helen put on her purple dress and dancing shoes and discovered the powerful magnetism of her own sexual desire, a whole new world opened up for her, one in which she could have some control.

Helen became a wandering princess, closer to her fairy grandmother's way. She seems to have had a great deal of fun, a time of discovery, an antidote to the claustrophobic family environment. But with motherhood came much pain and disillusionment with her partner, which plunged Helen into a depression reminiscent of her mother's when she was confined in the castle. She tells us that she had forgotten to honour the dark within her, and this is the result.

The dark may not always represent the shadow side, and even when it does, it can also be the way to the soul. We may not care for this part of ourselves, but it is wise to respect it, as the selkie or the serpent woman does. In the gospel of St Thomas, in *The Gnostic Gospels*, Jesus said: 'If you bring forth that which is within you, what is within you will save you. If you do not bring forth that which is in you, it will destroy you.' (From *The Gnostic Gospels*, by Elaine Pagels). We must take this to refer not only to our recognized talents, but also to our shadow.

The rabbit

Regression usually occurs within depression, and Helen describes this well, the frightened rabbit of her story depicting the terrified child at last finding some expression of her feelings. She had a powerful dream at this time:

Rabbit in a hutch

'There are two sisters who live with their mother; a dark haired sister and a fair haired one. The dark haired sister is mad, out of her mind, dangerous, and unpredictable. She has a knife, and she begins to stab her mother repeatedly in the head. Outside there is a rabbit that has grown so large it has filled the whole hutch. I feel so sorry for it, just lying there, accepting its surroundings.'

Depression, terrible though it is, can be a way through. It invites us to dig deeper into and come to terms with both our past and our depths. Often it holds us there, giving us no choice. People who are caught in depression need help to find their way through, rather than up and out of it. If they can find the courage to go even further down, to the root cause of this pain, they will find the seeds of their own healing. Helen feels that she was on the edge of a nervous breakdown, no longer able to contain her feelings and symptoms, when she first went to see a therapist. Just as the dream rabbit had grown to fill the whole hutch, so Helen's feelings had grown to become unmanageable. Starting therapy takes courage, for therapy has been called the talking cure. After just one session, Helen felt that something had changed; that she had been given a key, the key that was to unlock the door to her depression.

The stars

Astrology became a bridge between old and new, the inner and outer worlds, and the stars in her story became symbols of Helen's love of both astrology and dreams, which led her to me. Here is a star dream which she had at that time:

Stars at night

'*A man whom I know is driving me in a car. In waking, this man is cold and withholding. We go to a large country inn. Although it is dark, I know this is a beautiful place set in beautiful surroundings. There is something large and quite magnificent about the place, and a sense that I know it from long ago.*

'*I get out of the car and I am overwhelmed as I am met with a fantastic view of a clear night sky and the stars shining down. Because we are on a hill I can see more of the sky than I would normally be able to. It is truly wondrous. I feel so much love for the universe. I go into the pub. It is cosy and bright. My husband is sitting there on a long seat. He is wearing a brown flying jacket. He is ill but is getting better. I make my way towards him.*

'*I am in a place where a road passes overhead, and there are roads either side of us. The roads are deserted, and the one above us blocks out the sky. I am with an old boyfriend of mine. It is dark and cold and depressing, with lots of rubbish, a really ugly concrete place. He has his head down. I know there is something terribly wrong with him. I can come and go, but I think this is where he has ended up living.*'

The men

Helen's appreciation of the starry sky is somewhat overshadowed by the images of the men in this dream. It is only when she gets out of the car, driven by a man she knows to be cold and withholding in waking, that Helen can be inspired by the wonderful canopy of the night sky. He doesn't seem to share her delight as she's alone at this point.

Then there is her husband, the prince Helen had met and married in the early days of her dreamwork course. It is no coincidence that in the dream he is in the pub. Sadly, his 'illness' is his addiction, the same as her father's. When the dream of happy ever after fell apart and she recognized that she had in effect married her father, or at least married another alcoholic, Helen recognized how difficult it is to truly break the spell.

The third man, the old boyfriend, lives in a dark depressing place that Helen can move in and out of, but where he has become stuck. Clearly he is in no state to support her – the old way is not something she can really go back to.

Though he shares her father's addiction, Helen's hope seems to be with her husband as she moves towards him in the dream. Yet none of these men seems able to accompany Helen in her search for self-healing. It is a journey she must make alone.

Ending

Helen now has a fourth child, a daughter, who has been named 'Faith' in the tongue of her father's people. Faith is a healthy happy child and Helen is finding great joy and healing in caring for her. She also practises both astrology and dreamwork, knowing that at last her feet are planted firmly on a path that is right for her.

Finally, we would like to honour the struggle Helen still has with the family curse by sharing this dream. It ends on a sad but hopeful note.

Escape

'There are two children lying bound up with red rope next to a dark haired man who is asleep. One boy and one girl. I know exactly how these children are feeling. Utter fear. Fear is paralyzing them. I become the boy. We are lying here because, if the man found us escaping, things would be even worse than the fear we know now. Maybe I fear that he would kill us if he were to catch us.

'Some stronger impulse gets me, as the boy, to undo the rope that is keeping us prisoner. I know that if we stay there we will die, but not so violently. I free my sister and I, and get up and go into the other room. My mother is there and I want to take her with me.

'She is lying on the floor, a body without any bones. She tells us that we must go without her. She says it is too late for her, that we must leave her. I feel so sad, because I know that we cannot take her. We are too small and weak to drag her, even without her bones. I will say goodbye to her and leave through the open door behind me.'

Helen shows great courage in this dream, experiencing herself as a boy who is able to free himself and his sister. Here is her real strength, in the young inner Masculine who can act on her behalf, taking her away from the bondage of the family curse.

Try as she might, Helen cannot take her mother with her. It is too late for her. Boneless, she cannot stand up for herself in this situation. She has no backbone, is like a jelly, pliable, passive, lost in the collusion that alcoholism brings, which includes her own addiction. To free herself Helen must let go completely of her mother's way and make her own journey now, so that she can respond differently to her husband's drink problem.

Her courage shows through again in her agreeing to share her story with you too, telling the secrets, breaking the family taboo once more, and I am deeply grateful to her. She is learning all the time how to use her gifts even better, and maybe she will need to pass more of them on to her children when they have need. But the ghosts and ghouls do leave the garden when she shakes the rose bushes now, and she is finding more and more stars all the time!

conclusion

Weaving together the dream and waking experiences is a meaningful and creative task. It really connects us with our ancestors, with fairy tale traditions, and with the archetypes we encounter in mythology. It is a work of great scope and depth, bringing meaning into the daily round of life.

If you are daunted by the prospect of writing your story, why not begin with a practice run of rewriting a dream as if it were a story, which of course it is! Just move into the narrator role and tell it like it is. Or write the story of how you spent your day. Then develop onwards the story of your dream or your day, into a different ending of your choice. Play with it a little!

You may decide to emphasize and build a particular character, so that they become even more of what they are in the dream, so that you get a feel for what may turn out to be a sub-personality. Or perhaps you could try rewriting the dream from the viewpoint of one of the other characters. Try to get into their skin and experience the dream through their eyes – then write it from that place. This can be a very revealing exercise, yielding fresh insights into old situations.

No one but you need see anything that you write, so try not to write it as a performance piece but express yourself fully and flowingly. Let yourself be surprised by what comes.

In your work throughout this book you have learnt some of the skills I teach in my personal development course, The Dreamwork Experience. I have tried to give not only the techniques, but also some of the basics of the psychology behind the dream, to support you in your understanding of what dreams can bring.

Having followed the exercises, you will know by now that this isn't a superficial pass at dreamwork, or a quick fix. The skills you've learnt are skills for life. They don't even necessarily depend on the dream! You can use them in any waking situation, seeing it as if it were a dream and acting upon the insights you gain from this new way of seeing.

My years of experience of working with all kinds of people tell me that, if you continue to use these skills now, your life will start to make a lot more sense. You may begin to feel much more at home in your body, at ease with the natural flow of your feelings, and able to still your mind when it goes into the overdrive of anxiety.

Give yourself goals for keeping up the work, perhaps committing to carrying on for another three or six months. Then review your notes, looking at how the knowledge you have gained from this work has influenced your relationships and life events. Or you could focus on a particular aspect of your life, asking your Dream Maker to help you with it over the next few weeks and months, remembering to stay open and accepting of whatever your dreams bring.

If you really go for it this approach will work for you, but you should bear in mind that it is never about making change for change's sake, although you may choose to make great changes at times. It is more a matter of a slow, gradual growing into yourself that begins to show itself naturally in many subtle ways. Eventually your friends will begin to notice, and some of them will wonder at it, deciding that whatever it is, they want some too! Then you can invite them to share their dreams with you and help guide them on the first steps of their own journey. If you feel you'd like to do this, you could send for my information pack on setting up a peer group to share dreams in this way.

From your experience so far, you will already know that the dreamwork journey you are making is one of adventure and exploration, but above all, of self-healing. It can be difficult and demanding at times, yet it is also deeply rewarding and inspiring, becoming a true journey of the soul.

My thoughts and warmest wishes go with you, and I look forward to meeting you in the dreamworld at times. Travel well.

Be still and know who you truly are.

resources

For a list of Transformative Dreamwork practitioners and groups in your (UK) area, or for a resources pack to help you start your own dream group, please contact:

Maggie Peters, The Wing, Atcombe Court, South Woodchester, Near Stroud, Gloucestershire GL5 5ER, UK
Tel: +44 (0)1453 872709

If you cannot find a Transformative Dreamwork Practitioner near you, you may wish to seek out a therapist with a Transpersonal Psychology training. Details are available from:

The Centre for Transpersonal Psychology, Breasy Place, Anamcara Centre, 9 Burroughs Gardens, London NW4 4AU
Tel. +44 (0)20 8203 6671
http://www.transpersonalcentre.co.uk

The Institute of Transpersonal Psychology, 1069 E. Meadow Circle Palo Alto, CA 94303, USA
Tel: +001 (650) 493 4430
http://www.itp.edu

bibliography

Assagioli, Roberto *Psychosynthesis* Turnstone 1980

Bly, Robert *Iron John* Element 1991

Cooper, J C *An Illustrated Encyclopedia of Traditional Symbols* Thames & Hudson 1982

Corriere, Dr Richard; Hart, Dr Joseph *The Dream Makers* Bantam 1978 (out of print)

Estes, Clarissa Pinkola *Women who run with the Wolves* Rider 1992

Forward, Dr Susan; Buck, Craig *Toxic Parents – Overcoming their hurtful legacy and reclaiming your life* Bantam 1990

Graves, Robert (editor) *The Greek Myths* Penguin 1992

Greene, Liz *Astrology of Fate* Mandala 1985 (out of print)

Hillman, James; McLean, Margot *Dream Animals* Chronicle Books 1997

Jung, Carl *Man and His Symbols* Macmillan (Picador) 1990

Jung, Carl *Memories, Dreams, Reflections* HarperCollins (Fontana Press) 1995

Kalsched, Donald *The Inner World of Trauma – Archetypal Defenses of the Personal Spirit* Routledge 1996

Levine, Stephen *Who Dies?* Anchor Press/Doubleday 1982

McGuire, William *C. G. Jung Speaking* Princeton Univ. Press 1987

Moore, Robert; Gillette, Douglas *King, Warrior, Magician, Lover – Rediscovering the Archetypes of the Mature Masculine* Harper SanFrancisco 1992

Nakken, Craig *The Addictive Personality – Roots, Rituals and Recovery* Hazeldene 1998

Neumann, Erich *The Great Mother* Princeton Univ. Press 1972

New Larousse Encyclopedia of Mythology Hamlyn 1983

Parks, Penny *Rescuing the Inner Child – therapy for adults sexually abused as children* Human Horizons Series 1992

Woodman, Marion *The Pregnant Virgin* Inner City Books 1985

acknowledgements

I'd like to say a big thank you to Helena and Steve for suggesting to Gaia that I should be the one to write this book and to Helena especially for all her good work as editor. To Pip and all at Gaia for their support and encouragement. To my son Jake for his patience when I often needed help with the technology and, of course, to all those who have so generously and courageously allowed me to use their dreams, dreamwork material and stories – you know who you are! I'm so grateful to all of you.

Gaia Books would like to thank: Steve Hurrell for helping to prepare the ground in which the seed of this book has grown; Tanya Broomhead for her editorial assistance.

The diagrams in this book have been created by Maggie Peters, apart from Jung's Map of the Four Functions and Assagioli's Map of the Self.

The publishers have made every effort to trace the copyright holders of, and seek permission for, the quotes and extracts used in this book and apologise to anyone who has not been properly acknowledged.

index